the
Seeker's
Catechism

Michael Pennock

the
Seeker's
Catechism

the basics *of* catholicism

Now Referenced to the *Catechism of the Catholic Church*

ave maria press **AmP** notre dame, indiana

Nihil Obstat   Reverend Monsignor Michael Heintz, PhD, *Censor libroram*

Imprimatur   Most Reverend Kevin C. Rhoades
Bishop of Fort-Wayne–South Bend
January 31, 2012

© 1994, 2012 by Ave Maria Press, Inc., Notre Dame, IN 46556

Founded in 1865, Ave Maria Press is a ministry of the United States Province of Holy Cross.

www.avemariapress.com

Paperback ISBN-10: 1-59471-285-9   ISBN-13: 978-1-59471-285-2

E-book ISBN-10: 1-59471-349-9   ISBN-13: 978-1-59471-349-1

Cover image ©Travel Pictures Ltd/Super Stock

Cover design by Kristen Hornyak Bonelli.

Text design by David Scholtes.

Printed and bound in the United States of America.

Contents

Introduction

Leave your country, your kindred and your father's
house for a country that I shall show you; and I
shall make you a great nation, I shall bless you and
make your name famous; you are to be a blessing!

—Genesis 12:1–2

When Abram heard these words from God, he set out
on a journey of faith. Leaving his native land, he set
out with his wife, Sarai, neither one of them knowing where
the journey would lead them. They both had profound faith
in the promise that had been spoken, yet when they finally
arrived in the land of Canaan, they found themselves to be
"strangers in a strange land."

The faith of Abram and Sarai gave birth to a great nation,
and as Christians we are recipients of their legacy. Like them,
we are also strangers in a land that is not our permanent
home. We are on a lifelong journey that has as its ultimate
destination union with God who made and sustains us.

I offer this book to those who want to know more about
how the Catholic community journeys to God the Father. In
particular, I hope it will be useful for those who are discover-
ing for the first time the role that faith has in their own life
stories. Perhaps you have recently come to inquire about the
Catholic faith, or maybe you are returning to it after a long
time away. You may indeed feel like a "stranger in a strange
land." This book is intended to help you feel more at home
with what the Church believes and practices. I hope that in
the end it will inspire you to join or recommit yourself to the
Catholic faith and the spiritual riches it has to offer.

This book has its roots in the book *This Is Our Faith,* a
longer summary of the Catholic faith that was first published
in 1989. In an effort to provide a more concise book that

presented the most basic teachings of the Church, I selected key questions from *This Is Our Faith* and compiled shorter responses based on that text. These questions and their respective answers have been enriched by brief quotes from scripture, the *Catechism of the Catholic Church,* the documents of Vatican II, and papal encyclicals such as *The Splendor of Truth.* Each question and answer is correlated to pertinent reference numbers from the *Catechism of the Catholic Church* (CCC), with these numbers appearing on the right-hand margin, opposite the question itself. Those who desire a fuller treatment of any of the questions found in *The Seeker's Catechism* are encouraged to explore *This Is Our Faith.*

I invite you, the reader of this book, on a journey of faith sharing, deepening understanding, prayer, and reflection on the Catholic faith. My own prayer for all of us is that we come to love our Lord Jesus Christ even more. Let us never forget that the teachings of and about the Church have as their singular purpose to draw us closer to Christ Jesus and the mission to which he calls us in Baptism.

The Existence of God

Nearly everyone, at one time or another, has an incredible experience that profoundly alters his or her life's journey. At such times most of us turn to the divine, to God, and wonder about the hidden presence we have sensed in our hearts. Such experiences force us to ask questions about the meaning of life and the mystery of death.

Does God exist?
CCC 31–32; 34–35; 47

St. Paul and the Church assert that humans are able to discover the hidden God through rational thought because "ever since the creation of the world, the invisible existence of God and his everlasting power have been clearly seen by the mind's understanding of created things" (Romans 1:20). Belief in God is not unreasonable.

What does personal experience tell us about God?
CCC 27–30; 33; 46

Experience can guide us to God. Our feelings of dependency; our sense of wonder, awe, and joy; our openness to truth and beauty; and our feelings of being invited to do greater things than we are doing all speak of a God who has made us to discover and love him. Traditional arguments for God's existence include the following:

An unquenchable thirst for happiness. Did a creator make us with a hunger for happiness which nothing can completely satisfy? Might it be that God implanted in us a kind of homing device causing restlessness until we find him?

This yearning for total happiness points to a God who made us this way.

Sense of justice. We have a fundamental sense of moral goodness, a feeling that things will be reversed someday, that there is a power that will right all wrongs, if not in this life, then in the next.

Love. Love is a spiritual reality that is not explained by materiality. It must come from somewhere, ultimately from Love itself, the being we call God.

What does human history tell us about God?
CCC 51–53

Human history is a powerful argument for the existence of God. There seems to be an intelligence behind our evolving history. From the earliest times human beings have testified to the existence of God. An overwhelming majority of cultures have believed in some being who is greater than any of its members. We know *someone* is there, but God's true identity is not clear. We need divine help to know God as God really is.

What do demonstrations based on reason tell us about God?
CCC 31–32; 46

St. Thomas Aquinas, the great medieval theologian, summed up five so-called proofs for the existence of God. A key proof is the logical conclusion that all creatures must ultimately come from a cause that itself was not caused. This "Uncaused Cause" is God. Besides philosophical arguments, our own personal reflection on creation's beauty, immensity, and power can give us an awareness of a God who made all things and keeps them in existence.

Does God communicate with us?
CCC 51

God not only exists, but he freely chooses to communicate himself and the divine plan for salvation to us. The
Second Vatican Council (1962–1965) taught:

> In His goodness and wisdom, God chose to reveal
> Himself and to make known to us the hidden pur-
> pose of His will by which through Christ, the Word
> made flesh, man has access to the Father in the Holy
> Spirit and comes to share in the divine nature.

—Dogmatic Constitution on Divine Revelation, 2

What is divine revelation?
CCC 50–54

Christians believe God freely chose to communicate
himself and the divine plan of salvation to us. God did this
gradually by deeds and words inherently connected to each
other. This free gift of God's self-communication is known
as supernatural or divine revelation. God's self-disclosure
and invitation to a deeper life of love are purely gifts on
God's part.

> At many moments in the past and by many means,
> God spoke to our ancestors through the prophets;
> but in our own time, the final days, he has spoken
> to us in the person of his Son, whom he appointed
> heir of all things and through whom he made the
> ages.

—Hebrews 1:1–2

The story of God's self-disclosure, God's saving action
in history, is known as *salvation history.* Salvation history
reached its high point in the coming of Jesus, the fullness of
God's revelation. Jesus is the Word of God made flesh, the

Son of God who lived among us, taught us in human words and deeds about his Father, and completed the Father's work of salvation.

What is the Bible's role in salvation history?
CCC 74–87; 101–114; 121–125; 134–141

The story of salvation history continues on in our encounter with the Bible and in the Tradition of the Christian community. The Old Testament records God's teaching to the Jewish people and God's interactions in their history. The New Testament chronicles the life and teachings of Jesus and announces the Good News of God's plan of salvation for all people.

How does God help us respond to revelation?
CCC 25; 91–100; 142–144; 1813

We need to respond to God's self-communication and the revelation of God's plan for us. This response is known as *faith.* Faith, like revelation, is a free gift from God that gives us the conviction, commitment, and trust to believe in realities that we can neither see nor clearly prove.

Through this unearned gift of faith received at Baptism, we join a community of believers in the Lord Jesus who lives in our midst. Faith, hope, and charity make up the theological virtues.

- *Faith,* cooperating with divine grace, enables us to know God and believe what God reveals through the teaching of the Church. Through faith, we commit our whole person—intellect, will, words, and actions—to the God who reveals.

- *Hope* creates in us a desire for God. It enables us to trust firmly in God's loving plan for our salvation and that God will give us all that we need to attain it.
- *Charity* is God's own grace-filled life in us. It beckons us to live Christ's life of caring concern and service for others.

2

God: Our Loving Creator

In the Creed we profess belief in one God, the Father, the Almighty, the Creator. The Bible reveals that the very nature of God is love. God asks us to love in return as the way to happiness.

What does God reveal?
CCC 105–107; 121–123; 134–138

A primary way of listening to God is by reading and reflecting on the Bible. Catholics believe that the writings of the Old and New Testament are God's self-communication in human words:

> Through all the words of Sacred Scripture, God speaks only one single Word, his one utterance in whom he expresses himself completely.

> —*Catechism of the Catholic Church*, 102

The Bible, which literally means "the book," is more properly understood as a collection of books. This collection contains different kinds of literature such as poetry, history, religious myth or story, hymns, and proverbs. We believe that all the books of the Bible are inspired by God. By this we mean that through the guidance of the Holy Spirit the biblical writers accurately recorded what God wanted to communicate.

Catholics recognize forty-six books in the Old Testament. These officially accepted books comprise the *canon* (definitive list) of books in the Old Testament. The following points summarize some of the essential truths about God that these books reveal.

There is only one God. CCC 199–204; 210–211

When God chose to reveal himself to humans, he began with Abraham, whose descendants would become the Israelites. The Israelites came to call themselves "the Chosen People." Their history is one of *covenant* with God because they defined themselves in light of the solemn commitment God made with them. In return for God's great blessings and constant faithfulness, the Israelites (the Jewish people) were to obey God's law as summarized in the Ten Commandments. The most important aspect of the Israelites' response was to worship Yahweh and to testify to Yahweh as the one true God, the source of all being, the one who keeps everything in existence. All other gods were false and thus powerless.

We cannot know God. CCC 212–217; 268–271

God is essentially a mystery. God is totally other than creation. He is above and beyond it. God is eternal, unique, infinite, and all-powerful, unchanging, supremely holy, and utterly simple—a pure Spirit. Yet God is also present to and intimately joined with creation. For example, God formed and sustained the Chosen People, befriended prophets who spoke on his behalf, and promised a Messiah.

God is the Creator. CCC 279–308; 315–323; 337–349; 355–373; 380–384

God made all things out of nothing; creation is freely, generously, and wisely made to manifest and share God's glory. In the divine wisdom, God both sustains and rules the world. God created humanity in the divine image, able to think, choose, and love. Our human nature unites both the spiritual and material worlds. Created "male and female" in God's friendship, humans possess fundamental dignity. God created everything for man, but man in turn was created to serve and love God and to offer all creation back to him (CCC 358).

Evil exists because of our sin. CCC 374–379; 386–390; 396–412; 415–421

Because God created free beings and not mere puppets, humans had a chance to either accept or reject God's love from the beginning. Original sin is the unhappy result of Adam and Eve's having chosen to reject God. Their sin brought about disunity between God and humanity. The Book of Genesis tells us that this fractured relationship resulted in a corresponding disharmony between humans and the rest of creation, and our alienation from one another. This *condition of human frailty* is what we call "original sin."

God is loving, faithful, and true. CCC 214–221

The major theme of salvation history is God's loving faithfulness to his unfaithful creatures. God's love is manifested through deeds as well as words. God's deeds reflect a saving God—one who rescues the Israelites from the bondage of slavery in Egypt, one who sustains them in the desert, one who gives them a land and a king, one who keeps them alive in captivity, and one who returns them to their land.

The high point of God's loving concern is the promise to send a Messiah, a savior, who will restore humanity's proper relationship with God. In fulfillment of this promise God sent Jesus Christ, his only Son.

If God knows all, how can we have free will?
CCC 311

God's knowledge does not force us to do anything. God gave us freedom and respects that freedom even if it leads us away from God's love.

If God is good, why is there evil?
CCC 272–274; 309–314; 324

God does not create evil; evil is the absence of good. Rather, God permits evil. Evil enters the picture when free, intelligent creatures turn from God's love. We also believe that some evil in the universe results from fallen angels (devils) at odds with their Creator.

3

Jesus: Lord and Messiah

Jesus reveals that the way to his Father is to devote one's life to serving others and loving them without condition. His life, death, and resurrection have brought about our eternal salvation.

Jesus asked the apostles who people thought he was. Many of his contemporaries thought Jesus was a great prophet, or John the Baptist come back to life, or even the prophet Elijah. Peter answered in faith, "You are the Christ," the correct answer which would change his life forever (Mark 8:29). Jesus continues asking his followers today, "Who do you say I am?"

Did Jesus really exist?
CCC 423

Few people today doubt the historical existence of Jesus of Nazareth. Ancient Roman writers like Tacitus and Pliny the Younger and the Jewish historian Josephus take his existence for granted. A careful analysis of the gospels and what they record as the words of Jesus reveal that he must have existed. The teachings of Jesus bear the stamp of a memorable individual who taught with unique insight and authority.

The gospels are best described as summaries of faith that announce the Good News of salvation. The gospel authors (the four evangelists) were not primarily interested in recording the historical details of Jesus' life on earth, but rather in the good works he performed, the words of salvation he taught, and the meaning of his passion, death, resurrection, and glorification.

When were the gospels written?
CCC 126

The gospels were written over a period of about thirty-five years. Mark wrote around AD 65, Luke and Matthew between AD 75 and 85, and John in the last decade of the first century (90–100 AD). Each evangelist adapted his writing to the circumstances of his particular audience.

What do we know about Jesus' early life?
CCC 512–534; 561–564

Matthew and Luke wrote that Jesus was born of the Virgin Mary in Bethlehem. Luke records that Jesus accompanied Mary and Joseph to Jerusalem for the great religious feasts of the Jews. Luke also wrote that the twelve-year-old Jesus astounded the Temple teachers with his intelligence. Mark and John did not include details from the early life of Jesus.

When did his public ministry begin?
CCC 535–550

Jesus appears on the scene as an adult in the "fifteenth year of Tiberius Caesar's reign" (AD 27–28) when he was in his thirties. He launched his public ministry after being baptized in the Jordan River by John the Baptist.

What qualities of Jesus do the gospels reveal?
CCC 514–515

He was a healer. Jesus cured people of diseases and ailments. He cured lepers, the blind, the deaf, epileptics, the crippled, the possessed, and many others with various afflictions. Jesus' healings demonstrated God's love in concrete actions in behalf of his people—they showed that love has the power to overcome evil.

He was compassionate. The poor, the sinners, the abandoned, widows, and children all flocked to receive Jesus' love and understanding. He gave them what they really needed—the healing touch of God's forgiveness and the Good News that they were loved by God.

He was courageous. Jesus stood up to the false teachers of his day. He boldly preached the Father's will, knowing it would lead to his death.

He was humble. Jesus was poor, owned no possessions, and grew up in a place (Nazareth) that was not well thought of by the important—it was ridiculed as a backwater, even by Jesus' disciples.

He was self-giving. Jesus' love, his concern for all people, his miracles, his message of God's forgiveness, his preaching about God's kingdom—all of this got him in trouble with the religious and political leaders of his time who plotted to have him put to death. Jesus freely gave his life so that all people would be freed from the power of sin.

Did Jesus have brothers and sisters?
CCC 500–501

Catholics have long believed that Jesus did not have biological brothers and sisters and that Mary was always a virgin. These beliefs are based on both the biblical witness and the Tradition of the Church. The gospels say that Mary was a virgin and that Jesus was conceived by the power of the Holy Spirit (Matthew 1:20 and Luke 1:34). Church Tradition has always taught the perpetual virginity of Mary. The texts in the gospels that refer to Jesus' brothers use a Greek word that can also mean cousin or even distant relations of the same generation.

What do titles given to Jesus reveal about him?
CCC 430–455

- *Christ. Christ* is one of the most important titles given to Jesus. It is the Greek word for the Hebrew title *Messiah*, which means the "anointed one of Yahweh."

- *Suffering Servant.* Through his suffering and death, Jesus took on the burdens of his people and redeemed them.

- *Son of God.* Through his work and words, Jesus revealed himself to be the Son of God.

- *Lord.* In the Greek translation of the Old Testament, *Kyrios*, "Lord," is the usual way to indicate the divinity of Israel's God. When Christians began to use this title for Jesus in the New Testament writings, they were stating their conviction that Jesus was God, which is what we mean today when we proclaim Jesus as Lord.

- *Son of Man.* Jesus used this title for himself more than any other. It refers to Jesus as a human being and describes his role as the judge and the savior through whom God's reign will be established.

- *Word of God.* Human words reveal our thoughts and symbolically express what is hidden. In a similar way, the Word of God (Jesus) perfectly reveals God the Father. The doctrine of the *Incarnation* holds that the Word became flesh in Jesus. It is the mystery of the union of Christ's divine and human natures. "Belief in the true Incarnation of the Son of God is the distinctive sign of Christian faith" (CCC, 463).

How was the apostolic faith preserved?
CCC 688

The first few centuries of the Church were marked by growth in numbers, a deepening understanding of Jesus, and a greater grasp of the meaning of the paschal mystery. The Church Fathers—leading pastors, thinkers, and writers of the first centuries of Christianity—preserved the apostolic faith in Jesus as they explained his message to people of their day.

What is a heresy?
CCC 465–467

A heresy is a belief that is false or contradictory to Church teaching. During the first five centuries or so of Christianity, a number of heresies about Jesus arose in the Church. These heresies generally clustered into two main categories: some denied the humanity of Jesus, others denied his divinity.

How was heresy dealt with in the early Church?
CCC 90, 884, 891

The bishops called a series of ecumenical (worldwide) councils to carefully define the nature of Jesus Christ. The teachings of these councils state the classic dogmas of Catholics and other Christians about Jesus Christ, that he is true God and true man.

What did these councils teach?
CCC 464–483

These early ecumenical councils taught that:
- *Jesus is true God.* There was never a time when he was not God.

- *There is only one person in Christ, the divine person, the Word of God, the second person of the Blessed Trinity.* Thus, everything in Christ's human nature is to be attributed to his divine person—for example, his miracles and even his suffering and death.

- *Mary, by conceiving God's Son, is truly the Mother of God.*

- *Jesus has a divine nature and a human nature.* He is perfect in divinity and perfect in humanity.

- *Jesus has a human intellect and a human will.* Both are perfectly attuned and subject to his divine intellect and will, which he has in common with the Father and the Holy Spirit.

- *Jesus is a true human being, body and soul.* As such, he embodies the divine ways of God in a human way.

- *There exists a perfect union of the human and divine natures in the one person of Jesus.* Therefore, in Jesus, God truly shared our life with us.

- *Jesus, God-made-human, is our Savior.* By uniting ourselves to his death and resurrection through faith, we will share in the eternal life he has won for us.

- *Jesus will come in all his glory at the end of time to judge the living and the dead.*

4

Jesus: Teacher and Savior

Jesus met and touched many people. His touch always demanded some kind of response. The Lord continues to touch us today—through his Church, in his holy Word, in the sacraments, through other people. He continues to teach us. What he wants from us is change, true conversion of our hearts, minds, and actions to more closely align with his ways.

How did Jesus teach?
CCC 546

The Jesus of history was both a healer and a teacher. His teaching style was imaginative and provoked much interest. His whole life, every action and word he spoke, was his teaching. People were especially delighted with his parables—short stories with a religious message.

Does Jesus' teaching have meaning for today?
CCC 561

Christians believe that Jesus taught the most important message God ever delivered to us: the Good News of salvation, the message that saves us and wins for us eternal life. The gospels proclaim the meaning of the life, suffering, death, resurrection, and glorification of Jesus. But they also record the words of the Word of God. They show us the way to true happiness and unlock the meaning of life.

What did Jesus teach?
CCC 541–545; 551–553; 563; 567

God's kingdom is already here. The term *kingdom of God* (or *reign of God*) refers to God's active concern for us. It means that God's will is being done on earth as it is in heaven. It means that God's justice, peace, and love are helping to unite God's children here on earth. Jesus himself ushered in the kingdom. His healing of physical, emotional, and spiritual hurts was a sign of the kingdom. Although the kingdom started small and met resistance, it inevitably grew and continues to transform all humanity.

God is a loving Father. Jesus teaches that God is a loving Father whose love is tender and beyond anything we can fully comprehend. We can approach God with total confidence because God will provide for us and meet our most pressing needs.

God is merciful. Jesus proclaims that God forgives all sin. Because God is so forgiving, we should be joyful, happy people and imitate the Father by forgiving those who have hurt us.

God's love is for everyone. God's kingdom is open to all. It is a free gift; we cannot earn it. We show our appreciation when we love others. Jesus taught that the love of God and neighbor are one. And who is our neighbor? Everyone, even the stranger and our enemy.

Repentance and imitation of Jesus. If we want to enter the kingdom, we must turn from our sins and put on the mind of Jesus Christ. We must believe that Jesus is God's Son and become his disciples. We must be light to the world, allowing the Lord to shine through us by living lives of charity. What we do to others, especially the "least of these," we do to the Lord.

The Lord is with us. Jesus promised that he would be with us until the end of time. He sent us the Holy Spirit who unites us in love to the Father and the Son and to all our brothers and sisters. The Spirit—the living God who dwells within us—guides us, strengthens us, and sanctifies us as we try to follow in the Lord's footsteps.

To accept Jesus is to accept the cross. To follow Jesus into the kingdom means to do the will of God. Doing God's will involves self-denial and sacrifice. But Jesus promised that we will also share in the peace and joy of the resurrection. A life of service means dying to selfishness, but leads to an eternal life of joy.

Why do we call Jesus our Savior?
CCC 456–463

Christians hold that Jesus Christ is the fullness of God's revelation. Everything that Jesus said and did revealed God. The words he spoke were from the Father, living in him, doing his work. He came to bring salvation. The very name *Jesus* means "God saves," thus expressing our Lord's identity *and* mission.

What is salvation?
CCC 457

Salvation refers to the good that God intends for us. It is the mending of broken relationships, which keep us from being whole and at one with God and with our neighbor. It is the showering of God's blessings, the forgiveness of our sins, and the reconciliation of all creation to God. Salvation can refer to God's saving activity at work in both individual lives and within the whole of humanity.

What is the meaning of the passion and death of Jesus?
CCC 599–623

The birth, life, and teaching of Jesus are summed up in his passion and death on the Cross. Jesus freely entered into human suffering and death in order that humanity would be freed from the bondage of sin and death. His fidelity to his Father's will led him to a life of radical self-giving and, in the end, of total self-sacrifice.

The death of Jesus would be a tragic ending to the gospels except for the unparalleled fact of his resurrection. Through the death and resurrection of Jesus Christ, death itself died and all humanity was reconciled to God.

What is the meaning of the Resurrection?
CCC 638–653; 656–657

The scriptures tell us that God raised Jesus from the dead and the Lord appeared to his close followers. He sent the Holy Spirit to them as a guide and advocate. He commissioned his disciples to go out and continue the work he had begun: to preach the forgiveness of sin and the Good News that sin and death had been conquered. Jesus' resurrection confirmed his teachings, life, and promises; underscored his divinity; opened a new life for us; brought about our adoption into God's family; and laid the foundation for our own future resurrection.

What is the paschal mystery?
CCC 654–655; 658

The paschal mystery refers to Jesus' passion, death, resurrection, and glorification. Through these key events of our salvation, Jesus redeemed us from slavery to sin. He shares his life with us and through the Holy Spirit instructs us that love of God and neighbor is the vocation of all who belong to God's family.

5

The Holy Spirit: The Power of Love

Christians believe in the active presence of the Holy Spirit whose life-giving friendship works for us until the end of time. The Spirit transforms our lives from within. The Spirit's gifts enable us to accomplish God's saving work for others and the world in which we live. The Spirit is the mystery of God's love alive in the world.

What does **spirit** *mean?*
CCC 691

A common philosophical definition describes *spirit* as "the life force of living beings." Without spirit, there is no enthusiasm, no life.

Christians refer to God as spirit. We believe that the Holy Spirit is the third person of the Blessed Trinity, the Spirit of the Father with whom Jesus is filled. The Holy Spirit is the Father and Son's love, a gift to all of Jesus' followers.

What does the New Testament say about the Holy Spirit?
CCC 689–693; 717–730; 743; 745–746

Both the Acts of the Apostles and St. Paul's letters make many references to the Holy Spirit. The gospels also contain important references. John the Baptist is filled with the Spirit in his mother's womb. His parents, Elizabeth and Zechariah, are also filled with the Spirit. The Spirit overshadows the Virgin Mary at the time of the Lord's conception and is present at his Baptism, during the time of his desert temptations, throughout his teaching and healing ministries, and during his passion and death. Jesus also taught about the Spirit—for example, to Nicodemus (John 3:5–8) and to the Samaritan woman (John 4:10, 14, 23–24). Finally, it was through the Spirit that the Father raised Jesus from the dead.

The Holy Spirit is the very presence of the risen, glorified Lord, the Spirit of Love who exists with the Father and Son from all eternity. The Holy Spirit helps Christians on the great mission of continuing Jesus' work of forgiveness and reconciliation. The gift of the Holy Spirit enabled the apostles, and enables us, to know and to love Jesus in a new way.

Does the Spirit appear in the Old Testament?
CCC 702–716

The writers of the Old Testament also refer to the *Spirit* of God, but for them it has the meaning "wind" and "breath"—the breath that gives life. They also describe the Spirit of Yahweh in personal terms—guiding, instructing, causing people to rest. They treat God's Spirit as action rather than person. God's Spirit (wind) creates the earth by sweeping over the watery void (Genesis 1:1–2); God creates humans by breathing his Spirit into their nostrils (Genesis 2:7). The Spirit also enables the prophets to speak on God's behalf. The Old Testament tells us that God's Spirit will help God's people keep the Law and that it will be poured out on all people when the Messiah comes.

What are some images of the Spirit?
CCC 694–701

In Christian art the Holy Spirit is most often depicted as a dove—a symbol of peace, purity, and God's mysterious presence. The Bible uses other images—among them wind, fire, tongues of fire, and water—when it speaks of the Spirit's mysterious but real presence.

Wind. A driving wind signaled the coming of the Holy Spirit at Pentecost. Genesis also speaks of God's Spirit hovering over the watery chaos at the time of the creation of the world. Wind is a powerful image—something invisible but with quite evident effects. The image of Spirit as wind underscores the life and freedom given God's people through the Holy Spirit.

Fire. Fire evokes images of light, warmth, transformation or purification, power, mystery. The Old Testament refers to God as a consuming fire, even appearing to Moses in a burning bush. Pillars of fire guided the Israelites through the desert at night and symbolized Yahweh's judgment on the Chosen People. It purified the holy and destroyed the wicked.

Jesus refers to himself as the light of the world and calls on his disciples to be light as well. The Spirit is the inner light who gives us the capacity to encounter the vibrant life of the Trinity.

Tongues of Fire. The tongue is an organ of speech. Filled with the Holy Spirit, Jesus spoke for God; his words were the Father's words. When tongues of fire descended on the apostles, they were given the power to preach the truth about Jesus. And they were understood, even by people who did not speak their language. The Holy Spirit unifies, breaking down the barriers between individuals and among the people and God.

Water. Genesis reminds us of two important functions of water: destruction and life. God created out of the watery chaos, and when people sinned, God cleansed the earth with a great flood. Yahweh led the Chosen People to springs of water in the desert. In Baptism, water symbolizes death to a life of sin and a rebirth to an eternal life. Baptism represents initiation into the Body of Christ and bestows the gift of the Holy Spirit.

What is grace?
CCC 773–736; 742

Grace is the gift of the Holy Spirit that makes us children of God and brothers and sisters to one another. Grace is a share in God's own life.

Sanctifying grace is the gift of divine life in us who have been made holy by rebirth in Baptism and union with the Holy Spirit. It enables us to participate in God's own life and become the "image and likeness" of God, as we are called to be.

Actual grace is God's help to do good and avoid evil in the concrete circumstances of our individual lives. The Holy Spirit living in each of us calls us to act as God's children and helps us live a Spirit-filled life.

What are the gifts and fruits of the Spirit?
CCC 1830–1832

The Holy Spirit showers us with many gifts to accomplish God's work. The Spirit teaches us to pray and grants us seven gifts needed for a Christian life: *wisdom, understanding, right judgment, courage, knowledge, reverence,* and *wonder and awe in God's presence.* The Spirit gives each of us special gifts needed to build up the Lord's body. Some of us are called to be prophets, others to proclaim the Good News, some to heal, others to minister and teach.

The Holy Spirit makes us holy. The Spirit is the source of the good that we see in those who are alive in Christ. The fruits of the Holy Spirit—*love, joy, peace, patient endurance, kindness, generosity, faith, mildness,* and *chastity*—are the signs and sources of our happiness.

How do we experience the Spirit today?
CCC 688

We experience the Holy Spirit in the Church, the Body of Christ. The Spirit speaks to us through the Bible, in Tradition, and in the Church's teaching authority—the Magisterium, which guides us in living Christlike lives. We also experience the Holy Spirit in the words and symbols of the sacraments, in prayer, in the gifts and ministries that build up the Church, in the signs of apostolic and missionary life, and in the witness of the saints.

> The mission of Christ and the Holy Spirit is brought to completion in the Church, which is the Body of Christ and the Temple of the Holy Spirit.
>
> —*Catechism of the Catholic Church*, 737

6

The Blessed Trinity: Unity in Community

Christians believe that God is as a *Trinity* of persons—the Father, the Son, and the Holy Spirit. The Blessed Trinity is the central doctrine of Catholic faith from which other teachings are derived.

Who is God?
CCC 210–221

When Moses asked God for his name, God responded, *Yahweh*, which means "I am who am." This means, simply, Yahweh is *being* itself.

What does Jesus teach us of God the Father?
CCC 238–242

Jesus addresses God as *Abba*, a term of endearment that means "loving Father." Jesus tells the apostles the Good News that they—and we—can address God as *Abba* too. Jesus taught that the Father loves us in a way that is beyond our comprehension. The Father loves immeasurably and unconditionally. We cannot earn this love; it is a gift showered on good and evil people alike.

Our loving Father knows our needs and will give us what is good. St. Paul reminds us that the Father creates all things and wills the salvation of everyone through his Son.

The idea of God as Mother also adds to our understanding of God's love for us. A good mother tenderly protects, unblinkingly forgives, and unconditionally accepts her child. Every child who experiences the love of a faithful parent knows that it is the most natural, available, compassionate, and serving kind of love known to us. God's love is exactly like that.

Thinking about God as Mother or Father is helpful, for God embodies all the positive qualities we associate with both fathers and mothers—creativity, sustenance, nurture, guidance, availability, and love. But God possesses these without limit and does not bear the limitations of being male or female. God's love is unimaginably greater than the love of any human father or mother.

What do we know of God the Son?
CCC 240–242

Christians believe that Jesus is both the human face of God and the divine face of humanity. Jesus called God "Father" and related to him in a unique way. He taught that only the Son knows the Father, that all that the Father has is his, that the Father has given him all power, and that his words are the words of the Father who sent him. If we know Jesus, we know the Father. Everything about Jesus reveals the Father.

What do we know of God the Holy Spirit?
CCC 243–244

The Spirit was with Jesus throughout his ministry. Jesus promised to send the Spirit to his followers so that they might continue his mission in the world. He promised that the Spirit of truth and love would take up dwelling among God's people. As the Spirit empowered the followers of Jesus on Pentecost, the Spirit attracts us to the Son so that we might know him as our Lord and Savior. The Spirit enables us to proclaim that God is our Father. And the Spirit is the source of all good gifts given us by our gracious, loving God.

The mystery of the Most Holy Trinity is the central mystery of Christian faith and life. It is the mystery of God in himself. It is therefore the source of all other mysteries of faith, the light that enlightens them, and the most fundamental and essential teaching in the "hierarchy of the truths of the faith."

—*Catechism of the Catholic Church*, 234

How does the Trinity relate to us?
CCC 236–237

We can never fully comprehend the doctrine of the Trinity. God is beyond even the deepest human understanding. But God knows us more intimately than we know ourselves. He chose to share in our humanity in the person of Jesus and to take up his dwelling in us through the Holy Spirit. Through contemplation on the doctrine of the Trinity, we catch a glimpse of God's own essence, which is love—the intimate relating of Father, Son, and Holy Spirit, three persons in one God.

God the Father creates all things and continues to give life and being to everything in creation. God the Son lived among us, taught us of the Father's love, and won for us eternal salvation. God the Holy Spirit is the Love of God who dwells in us and in the Church as the source of unity, courage, truth, and love for all humanity.

What are the relationships within the Trinity?
CCC 254–256

Another way to approach the mystery of the Trinity is to reflect on the three distinct divine persons: Father, Son, and Holy Spirit. But we must not think of the divine persons in the same way that we think of human persons. There are not three separate consciousnesses in God. There is only one simple being. There are not three separate intelligences or wills in the one God. When one person of the Trinity acts, the other two persons also act. Each person is distinct but does not act separately from the others. God is a communion, a perfect unity of love.

God acts as one, though we appropriate or attribute certain actions to each of the persons. For example, we attribute creation to the Father, redemption to the Son, and sanctification to the Holy Spirit.

Traditional Catholic teaching explains the relationships among the three persons of the Trinity this way:

> *The Father.* The first person of the Trinity is without origin. From all eternity he "begets" the Son, the second person of the Trinity.

> *The Son.* The Son is the Father's perfect, divine expression of himself, the Word of God. They are one, yet distinct.

> *The Holy Spirit.* The Father and Son love each other with an eternal, perfect, divine love. The love *proceeds* from the Father and the Son and is called the third person of the Trinity, the Holy Spirit. The Holy Spirit is the Spirit of Love between the Father and the Son; the Spirit binds them into a community of unity.

7

The Christian Community

Members of the community founded by Jesus Christ share common interests and work toward common goals. It is a family of believers formed in Jesus' name and sustained by the Holy Spirit. Christians are quite diverse and individually unique. But they do have something vital in common: By virtue of their Baptism into the Christian family, they come together as a community to acknowledge and celebrate the Lordship of Jesus Christ.

The Lord brings us together and unites us into his people in order to continue his work on earth. We are united in that work with our Christian brothers and sisters who have gone before us in death and with those who will come after us.

What is the Church?
CCC 751–752; 777

The Church is the community of those who acknowledge Jesus as Lord; it is a community of believers who live a sacramental life and who commit themselves to fellowship and service for the sake of God's reign. Above all else, it is the mystery of God's loving grace.

Because the Church is unlike any other human community, no one definition or description can exhaust its rich meaning. The Second Vatican Council used biblical images to describe the Church: mystery, the People of God, the Body of Christ, the sacrament of Jesus.

The Bible alludes to many other images of the Church— for example, a pilgrim people, the sheepfold, or cultivated field, Christ's bride, the heavenly Jerusalem, and the flock of Christ.

What does the Church as "mystery" mean?
CCC 770–773; 779

St. Augustine defined a mystery as "a visible sign of some invisible grace." To call the Church a mystery is to say that the invisible, almighty God is working through this faith community, this institution that exists to continue the saving work of Jesus Christ.

What does the Church as the "People of God" mean?
CCC 781–786; 802–804

The image of the Church as the People of God has its roots in the Old Testament covenant between God and Israel. In the Old Testament covenant, God did not merely save, sanctify, and bless the individual Israelites. God formed them into a loving *community*. In the same way, each individual Christian, a temple of the Holy Spirit, is called into a *fellowship* of life, love, and truth with fellow believers—the Church.

The People of God are those of us who are baptized and acknowledge that Jesus Christ is Lord and Savior. Our mission is to live our lives in such a way that the Lord's light shines forth in the world through us. When we love one another, God's love can be seen.

Is the Church the same as God's reign?
CCC 763–764; 769; 782

God's reign, his saving activity in human history, which draws all people to him, is different from the Church. The Church includes only baptized members. The reign of God extends to all people who are saved for all time. But the Church and the reign of God are intimately connected.

The Church is the initial budding of the reign of God; its members work on its behalf in an explicit, conscious way.

The full flowering of this reign will take place at human history.

What does the Church as "Body of Christ" mean?
CCC 787–796; 805–808

The important image of the Church as "Body of Christ" can be traced to St. Paul, who wrote, "Now Christ's body is yourselves, each of you with a part to play in the whole" (1 Corinthians 12:27). Christ is the head of the body; we are its members. We become incorporated into the body through Baptism, and the Holy Spirit unites us into one body.

The risen, glorified Lord is present in the world today through Christians. We are his hands, his loving touch, his understanding glance, his sympathetic word of comfort to the lonely and suffering, his instrument used to preach the Good News of salvation.

Understanding the Church as the Body of Christ also underscores the dignity of each individual member. Just as each member of a person's physical body has a specific and important function to play, so, too, in the Church each member has a specific and important role to play.

> The Church is the Bride of Christ; he loved her and handed himself over for her. He has purified her by his blood and made her the fruitful mother of all God's children.
>
> The Church is the Temple of the Holy Spirit. The Spirit is the soul, as it were, of the Mystical Body, the source of its life, of its unity in diversity, and of the riches of its gifts and charisms.
>
> —*Catechism of the Catholic Church*, 808–809

Is the Church perfect?
CCC 853

...ans love, they build up the Body of Christ. ...rch includes a human as well as a divine ...hurch sins. The story of the Christian peo- ...e are both holy and sinful. We are a pilgrim people, a people on our way to total union with God. We are, of course, not yet perfect.

What does the Church as "Sacrament of Jesus" mean?
CCC 774–776; 780

A sacrament is a special kind of sign or symbol. A symbol, by definition, is something concrete that points to another reality. A sacrament is also an "efficacious symbol." That means it brings about what it points to; it embodies the very reality that it represents. Thus it is accurate to say that Jesus is the sacrament of God's love. Jesus not only points to God; he is God. He not only symbolizes God's love; he is God's love. He is what he represents.

The Church points others to Christ and is at the same time the presence of Christ here on earth. It is an outward, visible sign of God's loving gift of himself in human history. Like other efficacious symbols, the Church must point to something. It must lead us to Christ who is united to people through the Church. The Church helps put us in touch with the Lord whom it represents.

How does the Church lead us to Christ?
CCC 767–768; 849–854

The Church is a sacrament of Christ when it presents the message of God's love in Jesus Christ; builds up the Christian community; serves all people, especially those in need; and worships God the Father through Jesus Christ in the Holy Spirit.

Message. Down through the centuries the Church has announced the Good News that the God of love invites all people to the fullness of life. The Church must continue to preach this message to all people everywhere.

Community. For the Church to be an effective and credible sign of the Gospel, others must be able to see in the Church a community united by faith, hope, and love. If nonbelievers see in Christians loving, caring people, they naturally take notice and ask themselves what this group stands for.

Service. The third task of the Church is service. Jesus showed us the way when he took off his cloak and washed the apostles' feet at the Last Supper. A Christian should serve or minister to the needs of others. The Church must witness to God's love by translating its words of love into concrete acts of service for all.

Worship. Entrusted to the Church are the means of sanctification, especially the sacred mysteries—the sacraments. The celebration of the Eucharist is a special moment in the life of the Church because it celebrates and creates Christian community. It enables members of the Church to become Christ for others.

8

The Church: Its Mission and Nature

Community, service, and worship summarize our Christ-given mission. This is why the Lord wants each individual member of his body to be a messenger of the Gospel, by building up the Christian community, serving others, acting in behalf of justice, and worshipping God. Another way of looking at our mission is through the roles of priest, prophet, and king. The Church as a whole has the duty to continue the priestly, prophetic, and kingly roles assumed by Jesus himself. Each Christian shares in these roles in his or her particular life circumstance.

How does the Church function as prophet?
CCC 904–906; 942

A prophet is someone who speaks the Word of God. All Church members share in the prophetic mission of Jesus. Because we are baptized, Jesus asks us to witness to his truth in words and actions. "Lay people also fulfill their prophetic mission by evangelization, 'that is, the proclamation of Christ by word and testimony of life'" (CCC, 905).

What is the role of the Church's hierarchy?
CCC 874–882; 936–939

The Church's leadership is also empowered with the gift of prophecy. Jesus entrusted to his Church the task of authentically and truthfully proclaiming the Word as it appears in scripture and Tradition.

The Church has been led through the centuries by the Holy Spirit. The Spirit helps the Church authentically recognize and hand on what is essential to the Christian life. The pope, bishops, and pastors continue the ministry of Peter and the apostles, who were singled out by the Lord during his lifetime to continue his work on earth. The Church's leadership helps preserve authentic tradition and proclaim the true Gospel.

Catholics believe that the pope is the successor of St. Peter. As the head of the bishops—the successors of the apostles—the pope has primacy over the whole Church. The pope and the bishops form a single entity called the college of bishops. The bishops, in communion with one another and with the pope, must teach truthfully the Word of God. The pope's special role is to be a sign of unity when the bishops speak as one. He speaks with the bishops as the voice of Jesus Christ alive in the Church.

How does the Church teach?
CCC 892; 935

Normally the pope and bishops teach through the ordinary *magisterium* of the Church. *Magisterium* refers to the office of teaching in the Church, which the Lord gave to the apostles and their successors. Catholics recognize the primacy of the pope, bishops, pastors, and priests in the teaching mission of the Church.

> The mission of the magisterium is linked to the definitive nature of the covenant established by God with his people in Christ. It is this magisterium's task to preserve God's people from deviations and defections and to guarantee them the objective possibility of professing the true faith without error.
>
> —*Catechism of the Catholic Church*, 890

What is infallibility?
CCC 888–890

Based on our Lord's promise that the Church could not go astray because of his continuous presence, Catholics believe that on essential matters of faith and morals the Church is *infallible.* This is the belief that a certain doctrine (teaching) is free of error. This kind of teaching is rare, and there does not exist a complete and definitive list of all Church documents considered to be infallible.

What is papal infallibility?
CCC 891

The pope speaks infallibly when he teaches under the following conditions:

- as the visible head of the whole Church,
- to all Catholics,
- on a matter of faith or morals,
- intending to use his full authority in an unchangeable decision.

Papal infallibility refers solely to the pope's power or gift as successor of Peter to correctly teach Christ's revelation, especially when it is attacked or denied and leads to confusion among God's people. The pope's personal opinions and beliefs, like any person's, can be wrong. In addition, because the pope is human, he can sin and make mistakes, even in the way he governs the Church. Like all gifts of the Holy Spirit, infallibility is meant to build up the Body of Christ and give us access to the truth of Christ.

What is the Church's role as priest?
CCC 893; 901–903; 941

The Church leads others to sanctification through its role as priest. All Christians share in the common priesthood of Jesus in different ways. Some are called to act as official teachers, others to preside at the eucharistic table and to forgive sins in our Lord's name. Though only some are called to the ministerial priesthood through the Sacrament of Holy Orders (ordination), everyone in the Church—clergy and laity alike—shares the baptismal call to holiness, commonly called the "priesthood of the baptized." It is a great gift to be a member of priesthood of the baptized, but we should always remember that the measure of our personal greatness in God's eyes lies not in which gifts we have been given, but rather in the intensity with which we use those gifts in the love we bear for God and others.

What do we mean by the Church as "king"?
CCC 894–896; 908–913; 943

When we think of a king, we think of a ruler, an authority figure. Jesus reminds us that all authority resides in him. The Lord has chosen to share his authority with shepherds in the Church. He shares his teaching authority in a special way with the pope, bishops, and pastors. He also shares his ruling authority. The exercise of authority in the Church has but one purpose: the growth of faith and holiness among all the faithful.

The Church's governance must be carried out with humility, love, and compassion. The Church's standards must be those of Christ, never the standards of worldly rulers. The model of Church as king must be that of a serving king. As a constant reminder of this truth, Pope John Paul II took as his motto, "the servant of the servants of God."

What is the nature of the Church?
CCC 811

Four signs or marks have traditionally helped identify the Church's true nature: one, holy, catholic, and apostolic. These marks help to clarify and strengthen the faith of Catholics. But the signs are paradoxical in nature. They refer to the divine presence of Christ and the Holy Spirit working in the Church, yet the Church is made up of human beings who sometimes betray the very marks that should point to the Lord.

How is the Church one?
CCC 812–818; 820–866

The Church's oneness is rooted in the unity of the Blessed Trinity. There are three different kinds of unity in the Roman Catholic Church.

Unity of Creed. A creed is a body of beliefs. The creed is officially taught by the magisterium of the Church, and all Catholics are united in their belief.

Unity of Moral Teaching. The code of the Church refers to its moral teachings and their application to concrete contemporary issues. Catholics are united in the Church's ongoing quest to discover God's will in responding to moral issues.

Unity of Worship. The sacred liturgy—the Mass, the other sacraments, the Liturgy of the Hours, and other rites used on particular occasions such as the installation of a bishop or the consecration of a new church building—is celebrated around the world and has been a source of unity for Catholic worship down through the centuries.

Unity does not necessarily mean *uniformity.* Even though Catholics from around the world celebrate the same liturgy, there is room for cultural adaptation within the established structures.

How is the Church holy?
CCC 823–829; 867

God is the ultimate source of holiness in the Church, and Jesus Christ, the founder of the Church, is our model of holiness. In a sense, only God is holy, but because the Holy Spirit lives in the Church we can call the Church holy. We may also say the Church is holy because in it can be found "the fullness of the means of salvation." In other words, within the Church we find all that is necessary to become the persons God created us to be—holy and righteous, and one with him.

The Church possesses in a unique way the means necessary to help us achieve this full personhood: in the Word of God, which is found in the Bible; in Apostolic Tradition, the writings of great Church Fathers, saints, and theologians; in the teaching office of the Church; in the liturgical life of the Church; and in its devotional life.

How is the Church catholic?
CCC 830–835, 868

The word *catholic* means "universal." The Church is universal because Christ, who came to save all humanity, is in it. As St. Ignatius of Antioch observed, "Where there is Jesus Christ, there is the Catholic Church." The Church's universality manifests itself in three ways. First, the Church follows the Lord's command to teach all nations. The Church has reached out to all men and women at all times in all places. Second, the Church is catholic in the sense that it continues to teach all that Christ taught. Finally, *catholic* refers to fullness—a Catholic has access to the fullness of a faith relationship with Jesus Christ.

How is the Church apostolic?
CCC 857–865; 869

The present leadership of the Catholic Church can trace itself back to the first Christian leaders, the apostles. The bishops—successors to the apostles—in union with the pope continue to teach, sanctify, and guide the Church until Christ comes again. The Church is also apostolic in the sense that it professes the same doctrine and Christian way of life taught by the apostles. It has preserved the Good News of Jesus and his salvation and has not changed anything essential in his preaching or that of his closest disciples.

Can non-Christians be saved?
CCC 846–848

Traditionally Catholics have taught that the Church is necessary for salvation. Jesus himself taught the need for faith and Baptism. Consequently, the Church teaches that anyone, knowing "that the Catholic Church was made necessary by God through Jesus Christ, [who] would refuse to enter her or to remain in her could not be saved" (*Constitution on the Church*, 14).

What about those who have never heard of Jesus Christ? Can they be saved? The Church answers yes. God's reign includes those who are mysteriously drawn to it through the workings of the Holy Spirit in their lives. Their vocation is to seek the kingdom of God as they know it, and live as lovingly as they possibly can.

9

Catholic Morality: Living the Christian Life

Our key Catholic beliefs center on faith in Jesus Christ as Lord and Savior. But Christianity is more than a set of beliefs; it is a way of living. Christian faith must result in a life of loving service, or it is an empty faith. Christian morality helps us discover how we should live as a result of our faith in God's Word, which has been revealed to us in Jesus Christ and in his Church.

What is Christian morality?
CCC 1731–1738

Christian morality can be summed up in the word *responsibility.* There are two components to this term: *response* and *ability.* To what do we respond? Christian life is a response to God's freely given love and his gift of salvation offered to us through Jesus Christ. "Following Christ is thus the essential and primordial foundation of Christian morality" (Pope John Paul II, *The Splendor of Truth,* 19). Christian morality comes to the forefront when people say yes to God, when they freely respond to his love. The essence of Christian morality is, simply, love.

> You must love the Lord your God with all your
> heart, with all your soul, and with all your mind.
> This is the greatest and the first commandment. The
> second resembles it: You must love your neighbor
> as yourself.

—Matthew 22:37–39

The second aspect of Christian morality is the ability to respond to God—the ability to love and say yes to God.

This is also a gift, freely bestowed on us. It is part of what it means to be a human being. Human persons have basic dignity, which flows from their being created in God's image (with a soul). This implies that we can think and love and are in relationship to others in community. Our conscience aids us in a life directed toward God and other people.

What is a covenant?
CCC 54–67

When we reflect on the Christian life as a response to God's invitation to life and to love, we are stressing the *covenant* relationship between God and his children.

A covenant is the strongest possible pledge between two parties, typically of unequal rank, wherein certain commitments are made. The books of the Old Testament reveal Yahweh as a God who entered into a number of covenants with humans in general and the Jewish people in particular. In these covenants, Yahweh was always faithful. In return, God wanted the people to be faithful to the covenant. For the Jews, this meant living the *Torah,* or Law, as a way to respond to God. The Law, summarized in the Ten Commandments, was not seen by Jews as a random list of burdensome obligations to be tolerated, but rather as a way to live out the special identity bestowed on the Jewish people by God.

What is the New Testament covenant?
CCC 1718–1724

The most important covenant of all is the covenant of love God has made with humanity through his Son, Jesus. The New Testament covenant is a pledge in Christ's own blood. Jesus' death and resurrection seal our relationship with the Father. Christians live out this covenant by accepting God's love in Jesus Christ and responding to it. We respond through our Christian morality, which means living according to the Ten Commandments and the Sermon on the Mount as summarized in the Beatitudes.

> Christian morality consists in following Jesus Christ, in abandoning oneself to him, in letting oneself be transformed by his grace and renewed by his mercy, gifts which come to us in the living communion of his Church. . . . The one who loves Christ keeps his commandments (cf. John 14:15).
>
> —*The Splendor of Truth*, 119

What are the Ten Commandments?
CCC 2052–2082

The Ten Commandments are found in Exodus 20:2–17 and Deuteronomy 5:6–21.

1. I, the Lord, am your God. You shall not have other gods besides me.
2. You shall not take the name of the Lord, your God, in vain.
3. Remember to keep holy the Sabbath day.
4. Honor your father and your mother.
5. You shall not kill.
6. You shall not commit adultery.
7. You shall not steal.
8. You shall not bear false witness against your neighbor.
9. You shall not covet your neighbor's wife.
10. You shall not covet anything that belongs to your neighbor.

I, the Lord, am your God. You shall not have other gods besides me. The first commandment sets the priority for the Christian life. Simply put, friendship with God, which leads to eternal union with God, must be the focus and goal of our lives. There is always the temptation to make something else the be-all and end-all of our existence. Money, power, possessions, and pleasure are all good, but when we end up making these or similar accomplishments our primary goals, we have failed to recognize the one who created them, and this makes us unfaithful.

We honor the first commandment when we gratefully acknowledge, worship, and thank the source of our existence—God, our loving creator. The first commandment calls us to believe and hope in God and love God above everything.

The first commandment forbids any form of idolatry, superstition, astrology, divination, or spiritism.

You shall not take the name of the Lord, your God, in vain. The second commandment stresses our need to respect the Lord's name and to practice our religion humbly. The Christian realizes that what we say reflects who we are. Some things are sacred, including God's name, and our language and attitude toward our religion should be respectful. Thus, cursing—asking God to harm another—is wrong. Blasphemy—abusive or disrespectful remarks made against God—and swearing oaths falsely using God's name are also against the values of the second commandment.

Remember to keep holy the Sabbath day. Fidelity to God requires that we worship and adore God, in community with others. Our salvation is not something we work at in isolation. Catholics take seriously Jesus' mandate to break bread in his name. We gather weekly for community worship and set aside a day when we slow down from our other duties to rest, pray, and reflect. Catholics worship on Sunday to commemorate the day of the Lord's resurrection. Many begin the celebration of Sunday on Saturday evening since the liturgical day begins and ends with sundown. Catholics are encouraged to honor the Sabbath by refraining from unnecessary work, making time for loved ones, and engaging in other wholesome activity.

Honor your father and your mother. The covenant between Christians and God is reflected in the family. Just as God loves his children, so human parents should love and care for their children. And children should offer respect, obedience, courtesy, and gratitude to their parents. Likewise, brothers and sisters owe each other patience, friendship, and respect so that the family can be a harmonious community of love. This commandment also has wider social implications. All proper authority is deserving of our obedience and respect since all authority ultimately comes from God. And because authority comes from God, those in a position over others are obligated to exercise their authority with kindness and humility.

You shall not kill. God has given us the gift of life, and the fifth commandment stresses its sanctity. It condemns anything that assaults human life (for example, murder, suicide, or drug trafficking). The values of the fifth commandment include taking care of oneself—physically, mentally, and spiritually. Christians are also concerned about protecting the lives of others. Jesus showed that God's love extends in a special way to the weak and helpless. Thus, Christians should work for peace, justice, and life by combating war, poverty, prejudice, abortion, euthanasia, and other such social injustices.

You shall not commit adultery. Christian marriage is a powerful sign of covenanted love. Infidelity damages that love and threatens to destroy the covenant. The sixth commandment challenges us to respect the procreative powers with which God has blessed us. Sexual love is a share in God's own creative act. Acts which exploit others or which are indulged in selfishly distort God's intent. (See chapter 16 for more information on a Christian approach to sexuality.)

You shall not steal. Theft of any kind destroys trust. To steal is to break the human bonds needed for harmonious and peaceful living. The seventh commandment also forbids cheating and abuse of the environment. It reminds us to share the surplus goods we have been given with those who are in need. Not sharing with those who lack the very necessities of life is a serious failure to love.

You shall not bear false witness against your neighbor. To be honest is to witness to the truth. Lies, revenge, gossip, scandal, detraction (unnecessarily disclosing another's faults), and perjury all destroy the love that binds together the human community and all violate this commandment.

You shall not covet your neighbor's wife. You shall not covet anything that belongs to your neighbor. Covetousness is often motivated by lust, self-indulgence, envy, or greed. Uncontrolled desires in the areas of sex or material possessions can breed hatred, jealousy, and rivalry. These two commandments stress the importance of pure intentions and decent motives when relating to others. The actions that violate love usually flow from a desire that has not been channeled into appropriate interactions that respect human dignity.

What are the Beatitudes?
CCC 1716; 1725–1727

The Beatitudes summarize the way followers of Jesus should strive to live. They communicate the essence of New Testament morality found in the Sermon on the Mount (Matthew 5–7). The Beatitudes are "a sort of self-portrait of Christ"; they are "invitations to discipleship and communion of life with Christ" (Pope John Paul II, *The Splendor of Truth*, 16).

> How blessed are the poor in spirit: the kingdom of Heaven is theirs.
>
> Blessed are the gentle: they shall have the earth as inheritance.
>
> Blessed are those who mourn: they shall be comforted.
>
> Blessed are those who hunger and thirst for uprightness: they shall have their fill.
>
> Blessed are the merciful: they shall have mercy shown them.
>
> Blessed are the pure in heart: they shall see God.
>
> Blessed are the peacemakers: they shall be recognized as children of God.
>
> Blessed are those who are persecuted in the cause of uprightness: the kingdom of Heaven is theirs.
>
> —Matthew 5:3–10

How do we explain the Beatitudes?
CCC 1716–1717

How blessed are the poor in spirit: the kingdom of Heaven is theirs. In this beatitude Jesus is not praising poverty as such. Rather, he is saying that those who are deprived of material goods, power, prestige, and other signs of worldly success are left in a position of openness before God. They know they must trust God completely for everything. Jesus asks that we have that same poverty of spirit, that we place our trust and confidence in God alone.

Blessed are the gentle: they shall have the earth as inheritance. The gentle person is humble. He or she does not act out of jealousy or seek revenge when hurt and despised.

Blessed are those who mourn: they shall be comforted. The third beatitude gives us hope that in the midst of our difficulties we will eventually find consolation. We do not have to become bitter.

Blessed are those who hunger and thirst for uprightness: they shall have their fill. To "hunger and thirst for uprightness" means to seek divine justice. To seek divine justice means to seek a good relationship with the perfectly upright, just, and righteous One. Participation in Sunday Eucharist each week strengthens and renews this relationship. The Eucharist impels us to treat others with justice, giving them their due and making sure that everyone has access to those things necessary for a life of dignity.

Blessed are the merciful: they shall have mercy shown them. In the Our Father we ask God to forgive us as we forgive others. When we forgive those who have hurt us, even our enemies, we show all people that God is loving and merciful and that God cares for us all.

Blessed are the pure in heart: they shall see God. The pure in heart have a single-hearted commitment to God. Nothing should distract us from God. Money, job, family, friends, reputation are all good, but they should play a secondary role in our lives.

Blessed are the peacemakers: they shall be recognized as children of God. Living in love and peace is characteristic of being one of God's adopted children. Christians have the duty to unite those who are in strife, disharmony, and opposition by helping them realize our common brotherhood and sisterhood with Jesus Christ.

Blessed are those who are persecuted in the cause of uprightness: the kingdom of Heaven is theirs. There is no greater sign of union with our Lord than being willing to suffer for him. Jesus' words and deeds brought him misunderstanding and abuse. To be Christian means to be willing to stand up for our convictions, even if this means rejection, abuse, or martyrdom.

10

The Church and Social Justice

The Lord's people, his Church, are missionary. Our mission is threefold: to be the herald, the sign, and the servant of the Gospel. We herald the Good News when we proclaim Christ's resurrection. We are signs of the Gospel when we faithfully live as Jesus taught. We serve the Gospel when we witness to the message of God's saving love for the world by working on behalf of justice for all people.

How are social justice and Gospel love related?
CCC 1928–1933; 1943–1944

Social justice deals with the application of the Gospel to the structures, systems, and institutions of society. As stated in *Justice in the World*, a 1971 statement from the Synod of Bishops, "Love implies an absolute demand for justice, usually a recognition of the dignity and rights of one's neighbors." We cannot say we love if we do not respect and respond to the rights and basic needs of our neighbors. Authentic love of God and love of neighbor are inseparable realities.

In other words, to love means to give oneself to another. It is impossible to love without sharing with others what is due them in justice. Love can go beyond justice, however. Justice is simply the *minimal* human and Christian response to others. Love, if we are serious about becoming like Christ, requires going beyond justice.

What role has the Church played in justice issues?
CCC 2419–2425

Throughout its history the Church has attempted to show the link between the Gospel and the plight of the poor. The Catholic Church has often pioneered efforts on behalf of the poor and the powerless: home and foreign missions, hospitals and medical clinics, disaster relief agencies, orphanages, homes for unwed mothers, services for the elderly, agencies for young people, a massive educational apostolate.

There are those, however, who have criticized the Church for not taking a more active role in promoting peace and justice. Church leaders have at times neglected the social dimension of the Gospel while preaching to the poor and oppressed a quiet acceptance of their state in life.

In our day the Church has taken a leading role in the promotion of justice:

> Action on behalf of justice and participation in the transformation of the world fully appear to us as a constitutive dimension of the preaching of the Gospel, or in other words, of the Church's mission of the redemption of the human race and its liberation from every oppressive situation.

> —*Justice in the World*, Introduction

This important document makes it clear that working for justice in the world ranks with the celebration of the sacraments and the preaching of the Gospel as an essential ministry of the Church.

What are the basics of the Catholic social teaching?
CCC 2419–2449

In their pastoral message *A Century of Social Teaching: A Common Heritage, A Continuing Challenge,* the United States

Conference of Catholic Bishops outlined six basic themes
that undergird Catholic social teaching:

1. The Church upholds the life and dignity of the
    individual.

2. The Church recognizes that there are certain basic human
    rights with their corresponding duties.

3. The Church recognizes that human beings are by nature
    social and that God calls us to family, community, and
    service.

4. The Church recognizes the truth of human solidarity and
    that all humans belong to one family, God's family.

5. The Church upholds the dignity of work and the rights
    of workers.

6. The Church teaches a preferential option for the poor
    and vulnerable.

What is meant by "the dignity of the individual"?
CCC 27, 1700–1703

Catholic social teaching is rooted in the dignity of the
human person. Each of us images and reflects God. Jesus
loves and redeems all humans. All have basic dignity and are
"capable of knowing and loving their Creator" who made us
(*The Church in the Modern World*, 12). Our worth comes from
who we are as God's children, not what we do. Our worth
is not dependent on race, gender, age, or economic status.
Catholic social teaching requires us to judge every policy,
law, and institution according to how it enhances human
life and dignity.

What are our rights and duties?
CCC 1913–1917; 2415–2418; 2451–2452; 2456–2457

Justice demands that a society be organized in such a way so as to guarantee that everyone has the ability to participate in its political, cultural, and economic life. Basic human rights are prerequisites to living a life of dignity in community. Among the major human rights that have been discussed and defended in a number of Church documents are the following:

Economic rights
- right to life: food, shelter, clothing, and medical care
- right to work
- right to a just wage
- right to property

Political and social rights
- right to participate in government
- right to judicial protection
- right to assembly

Religious and cultural rights
- right to worship
- right to a basic education
- right to freedom of speech

Every right has a corresponding duty for each person to respect, foster, and fulfill. For example, the right to participate in government carries the duty to cast an informed vote in elections.

In what way are humans social beings?
CCC 1877–1882; 1890–1893

God created us as members of the human family. We are by nature social. From the beginning God created us for companionship. The progress of the human person and the advance of society are interdependent. We belong to three communities that are like concentric circles: the individual lives in the circle of the family, which is part of a larger circle, the nation, which is part of the largest circle, the world. These are the communities most often discussed in the Church's social teaching.

What is the call to human solidarity?
CCC 2437–2442

Our solidarity with each other and our world encompasses issues like world peace, global development, environmental issues, and international human rights. Violent conflict and the denial of human rights to people anywhere affect and diminish us all. We simply must hear the call of others, especially the most vulnerable members of the human family. Jesus united the love of God and love of neighbor and prayed for human solidarity: "May they all be one, just as, Father, you are in me and I am in you" (John 17:21).

What is the relationship between the dignity of work and the rights of workers?
CCC 2426–2436

Work helps us make a living, expresses our human dignity, and helps us participate in God's ongoing creation. Work must be for people, not people for work. We have the basic right to decent and productive work, fair wages, private property, and economic initiative. The Church has consistently upheld workers' rights to form unions and associations in their pursuit of their rights and dignity, as well as the belief that the economy exists to help people, not vice versa.

What is the "preferential option for the poor"?
CCC 2443–2449; 2461–2463

Catholic social teaching asks society this question: How are its most vulnerable members faring? Jesus taught that we must put the needs of the poor and vulnerable first. Pope John Paul II expressed well the link between justice and the love of the poor:

> Justice will never be fully attained unless people see in the poor person, who is asking for help in order to survive, not an annoyance or a burden, but an opportunity for showing kindness and a chance for greater enrichment. It is not enough to draw on the surplus good, which in fact our world abundantly produces; it requires above all a change of lifestyles, of models of production and consumption, and of the established structures of power which today govern societies.

—The One Hundredth Year, 58

11

Social Justice: Building on the Foundations

Catholic moral teaching is interested in social justice because social justice applies the Gospel command to respect and love others to the concrete realities of life. The Gospel is not meant to be a vague, idealistic statement with no connection to how people live their lives. Rather, it demands application to the social settings in which we find ourselves: families, nations, and the world.

What does the Church teach about the family?
CCC 1655–1658; 1666

The bedrock unit of any society is the family. Its special value lies in its willingness to affirm and love individuals, not for what they can accomplish or the possessions they own, but simply for who they are. Married couples model Christ's own love for the Church. His love is enduring and self-giving. Marriage is both love-sharing between the couple and life-giving. The twin values of life and love provide a strong foundation for the larger society.

What principles undergird Church teaching on national concerns?
CCC 1905–1917; 1924–1927

All nations must be concerned about social issues, problems, and rights in order to foster the common good. The topics discussed below—respect for the unborn, women in society, respect for racial and ethnic groups, employment, and poverty—are frequently addressed in papal documents and in the letters of national conferences of bishops.

What is the Church's stance regarding the unborn?
CCC 2268–2283; 2322–2325

Jesus taught in the strongest of terms the need to care for the weak and the helpless. For the sake of the common good, the fundamental right to life itself must be first recognized and then protected by law. Efforts to correct legal decisions that permit abortion on demand, for example, are one means to remedy the assault on human life.

Society also needs to offer help and assistance to those women who believe that abortion is the only real choice they have when faced with a crisis pregnancy. The Church should be in the forefront of offering necessary support to these women and their children during and after pregnancy. The Church must provide the strongest possible witness to its belief in human dignity by tending to the material, emotional, and spiritual needs of these families.

Respect and reverence for human life arise from the basic dignity of the human person made in God's image and likeness. Life is a most precious gift from God. Abortion is gravely wrong, as is any direct attack on human life like infanticide, euthanasia, and certain kinds of fetal experiments.

What does the Church teach about discrimination?
CCC 1934–1938; 1945–1947

Because God created each person with a human nature endowed with fundamental dignity and a common destiny, all people are, in essence, equal. Any form of discrimination, whether based on sex, race, color, socioeconomic condition, language, national origin, sexual orientation, or religion is immoral and contrary to God's love for each person.

Although all persons are equal in human dignity, we have different talents and abilities. These differences are part of God's plan, something we can never fully understand, especially if we have been especially gifted. Our duty is to generously share our gifts with others and work in a special way to fight against sinful inequalities.

What is the Church's stance on employment?
CCC 2426–2436; 2458–2460

The Church has spoken clearly on the rights of workers:

Every [person] has the right to work, to a chance to develop his qualities and his personality in the exercise of his profession, to equitable remuneration which will enable him and his family "to lead a worthy life on the material, social, cultural, and spiritual level" and to assistance in case of need arising from sickness or age.

—A Call to Action, 14

What does the Church teach about poverty?
CCC 2443–2449

The American bishops define poverty as "the lack of sufficient material resources required for a decent life" (*Economic Justice for All*, 173). The American bishops' pastoral letter on the economy makes a number of concrete recommendations on how the plight of the poor can be helped. These include raising the minimum wage, adjustments in the tax system to better meet the needs of the poor, major commitments to education and the eradication of illiteracy, better support of families so that both parents of young children are not forced to seek employment outside the home, and a thorough reform of the welfare system.

Consumerism leads to materialism, which in turn leaves people empty. The media contributes to the message that the more one has, the greater success one is. Consumerism,

which hurts the poor, makes people self-centered and fails
to fulfill their true human destiny.

> It is not wrong to want to live better; what is wrong
> is a style of life which is presumed to be better when
> it is directed toward "having" rather than "being"
> and which wants to have more, not in order to be
> more, but in order to spend life in enjoyment as an
> end in itself.

— Pope John Paul II, *The One Hundredth Year*, 36

What other social problems has the Church addressed?

- *Crime and criminals.* People have the right to live in peace
  and be protected from criminals. Societies should not only
  work at stricter law enforcement, but should also strive
  to root out the sources of much crime: poverty, injustice,
  and materialism.

  Prisoners, too, have rights: They have the right to protection from assault; the right to proper food, health care,
  and recreation; and the right to pursue other human goals
  such as education.

- *Migrant workers.* The condition of migrant workers is
  addressed in *Justice in the World*. These workers are especially vulnerable and frequently become the victims of
  discriminatory attitudes and oppressive living conditions.
  Emigrating to find work is sometimes a necessary evil,
  but "migration in search of work must in no way become
  an opportunity for financial or social exploitation" (*On
  Human Work,* 23).

- *Communications.* The people who control media have a
  "grave responsibility with respect to the truth of the information they spread, the needs and the reactions they gen-
  erate, and the values they put forward" (*A Call to Action,*

20). In this regard the American bishops suggest that the government can help create more wholesome societies by taking "constitutional steps to stem the flood of pornography, violence, and immorality in the entertainment media" (*To Live in Christ Jesus,* 30).

- *Environment.* When God entrusted the human race with the development of the created world, he made us stewards of his magnificent creation (Genesis 1:28–30). This is a tremendous responsibility. Yet today we have become more aware that we have exploited nature and that we now risk destroying it. Pollution, refuse, scarcity of vital natural resources, and new illnesses result from unchecked manufacturing and commercial practices that are fueled more by human selfishness and greed than by concern for our real needs. Responsibility demands careful planning, conservation, and an unselfish respect for the goods of this world.

What does the Church teach about world problems?
CCC 2437–2442

Our concern for the rights of others does not stop with the family or with our own nation. To follow Jesus means to love all people. The Christian in today's world must also show concern for the international community. Christian love and justice prompt us to extend care beyond our national borders.

The world community is in dire need of creative and cooperative efforts to address the problems of hunger, environmental pollution, population growth, disparity of wealth and resources, and the persistent threat of violence.

What is the Church's response to these global issues?
CCC 2304–2305

Pope John Paul II called on individuals, community leaders, societies, and entire nations to convert and turn away from greed and consumerism and to make a wholehearted commitment to work for the integral development of every human being. True development begins with love of God and love of neighbor, and love manifests itself in respect for all God's creatures. Of major concern to the Church in our day has been the right of nations to develop and become liberated from oppressive practices and situations that keep the poor in a state of life unworthy of human dignity.

A constant theme in papal teaching concerning developing nations has been the right of those nations and peoples to control and direct their own process of development. The right to develop includes economic growth as well as political, social, and economic participation in the process of development.

The Church likewise teaches that to be disciples of Jesus Christ means to be passionately devoted to peace. Peace is not merely the absence of war. It is an enterprise of justice and must be built up ceaselessly.

12

Sacraments: A Life of Grace

We need symbols because we are corporeal beings. We need signs that are perceptible to our senses to help express invisible realities such as love, respect, and reverence. We need to speak and hear loving words, give and receive gifts, shake hands, salute, and embrace, write and receive notes of appreciation, and use many other symbols and symbolic actions to express the most profound human experiences. This is true in our relationships with other people and it is true in our relationship with God.

Sacraments and the sacramental life are absolutely central to Catholic identity and belief. They provide us with rich symbols and rituals to express what we believe about God and our relationship to him. To reflect on their meaning and to appreciate what they represent—God's presence in the ordinary moments of our lives—is to grow in an understanding of what Catholics hold to be very precious. In a real sense, the sacraments are an embodiment of the Good News of God's love.

What is a sacrament?
CCC 1115–1116; 1131

A *sacrament* is an "efficacious sign"; that is, it is a sign (or symbol) that causes what it points to, what it represents. As we saw in chapter 7, this definition fits both Jesus and his Church. The seven sacraments are special actions of Christ working in the Church. They are effective, symbolic actions that not only point to God's life but actually convey it to the members of the Church. They bring about what they point to—the presence of Christ.

What are these symbols of God's love for us?
CCC 1113; 1119–1121; 1132

The Catholic Church recognizes seven sacraments. We believe that the Lord has left the Christian community with these seven signs of love that touch us during key moments of our lives. When we begin life, Baptism unites us with the risen Lord and with our fellow Christians. As we mature and begin to more fully accept and live the Christian life, Confirmation showers us with the strength of the Holy Spirit to live faithfully for the Lord. The Eucharist, the sacred meal that commemorates and reenacts the Lord's sacrifice on the Cross, symbolizes and brings about our union with God.

When we are guilty of sin and in need of reconciliation and forgiveness, we experience the Lord's forgiving love in the Sacrament of Penance. And in times of serious illness, the Anointing of the Sick gives us God's mercy, forgiveness, courage, and hope.

Jesus is with us as we live out our vocations. Those who are called to serve the Church as deacons, priests, or bishops are supported through the Sacrament of Holy Orders. Those called to the Sacrament of Marriage commit to being a visible sign of God's love through their fidelity toward one another.

What does a sacrament do?
CCC 1123–1124; 1130; 1133–1134

A sacrament makes visible the mystery of God's love for us.

> [Their purpose] is to sanctify, to build up the body
> of Christ, and finally, to give worship to God.
> Because they are signs, they also instruct. They not
> only presuppose faith, but by words and objects
> they also nourish, strengthen, and express it.

—*Constitution on the Sacred Liturgy*, 59

What is the traditional definition of sacrament?
CCC 1131; 1084

The *Catechism of the Catholic Church* (1131) reaffirms a classic definition of the term *sacrament*: "an efficacious sign of grace, instituted by Christ and entrusted to the Church, by which divine life is dispensed to us."

- *Efficacious sign.* St. Augustine defined a sacrament as a "visible sign of invisible grace." Through words and actions we can sense, experience, and come to believe spiritual realities that exist beyond our senses. We know that something important is happening behind these outward signs, which bring about what they point to. We are celebrating Christ's presence; God's friendship with his people is entering our lives.

- *Instituted by Christ and entrusted to the Church.* Jesus came to preach the Good News and establish his Father's kingdom. With the guidance and power of the Holy Spirit, the Church has developed the seven sacraments as special, unique signs whose purpose is to build up the kingdom of God. God's action, not human action, makes the sacraments what they are.

- *To confer grace, God's life, to us.* The purpose of the sacraments is to convey grace. *Grace* is a traditional Catholic term that refers to our participation in the life of God. Grace is God's free gift of friendship that enables us to live as his adopted daughters and sons.

Sacraments are not magic. They presuppose openness, faith, and cooperation on our part. We must respond to them and live the gift of God's life.

> The sacraments are perceptible signs (words and actions) accessible to our human nature. By action of Christ and the power of the Holy Spirit they

make present efficaciously the grace that they
signify.

—*Catechism of the Catholic Church*, 1084

What is liturgy?
CCC 1069; 1074–1075

Public worship of God is known as *liturgy,* from a Greek
word that means "the people's work." Liturgy includes the
celebration of Mass and the other sacraments, the Liturgy of
the Hours, and ceremonies or rites used for particular occasions such as the installation of a bishop or the dedication
of a new church. Christian liturgy uses words, actions, and
symbols to celebrate the presence of God in our midst. It
reminds us of who we are and how we are to live in relationship with our loving God. Through it we bless and worship
God as the source of all blessings.

It is the mystery of Christ that the Church proclaims
and celebrates in her liturgy so that the faithful may
live from it and bear witness to it in the world.

—*Catechism of the Catholic Church*, 1068

Liturgy is organized ritual activity. All rituals bring a
recognizable order to certain words, actions, and symbols
in order to create a meaningful celebration for a particular
group. The seven sacraments are important rituals of the
Church.

13

The Sacraments of Initiation

The Sacraments of Initiation help "gather in" God's people, incorporating them into the Body of Christ, the community of believers that is the Church. Like all sacraments, they commission God's chosen ones to be Christ for the world. These sacraments confer the life of Jesus and bestow the gift of the Spirit on the People of God so that they can continue the Lord's mission in word and deed to a world that is hungering for meaning and love.

What are the Sacraments of Initiation?
CCC 1214–1216; 1277

The Sacraments of Baptism, Confirmation, and Eucharist are known as the Sacraments of Initiation. Most American Catholics were baptized as infants, received First Communion around second or third grade, and were confirmed either in junior or senior high school. In early Christian times, most converts were adults who celebrated all three Sacraments of Initiation at one time after participating in a lengthy formation period—often three years—called the *catechumenate.* With the help and companionship of sponsors, these *catechumens* learned about the Christian faith and became disciplined in the Christian way of life through prayer, fasting, and self-denial. This ancient way of initiating adults into the Christian community has been revived over the last twenty-five years through the *Rite of Christian Initiation of Adults* (RCIA).

What is the RCIA?
CCC 1247–1249

The RCIA is a process by which individuals are baptized into the Catholic Church. It has four distinct periods during which catechumens are helped to prepare for initiation by learning about the faith and through prayer and spiritual direction. The progression from each period to the next is marked by a special rite. There are three primary rites and several minor ones.

- *Period 1: Pre-catechumenate.* The journey to Christian initiation begins with a period of inquiry called the pre-catechumenate. The inquirers share life experiences with Catholics, reflect on the scriptures, seek knowledge about the Catholic religion and its relationship to other Christian communities, and learn about Jesus Christ.

  The transition from this period to the next is marked by the *Rite of Acceptance.* Through this rite, inquirers ask for acceptance into the Catholic faith community and are joyfully accepted into the Church as candidates for Christian initiation. They then become known as *catechumens.*

- *Period 2: Catechumenate.* After the initial celebration of acceptance, the catechumens study the Christian faith more deeply (sometimes under the guidance of a sponsor, a caring role model). Catechumens grow familiar with the Christian way of life, study the scriptures, participate fully in the Liturgy of the Word at Sunday Masses, and begin to take an active role in the life of the parish community.

  The *Rite of Election* moves catechumens from the catechumenate to the next period of preparation. This rite begins with a sending forth from the parish at Mass and continues in a diocesan celebration, usually in the cathedral church. This Rite of Election includes a presentation of the candidates for initiation to the local bishop and an enrollment of their names in a special book. They are then known as *the elect* because they have been chosen by God and called by their local Catholic community to become full members of the Church.

- *Period 3: Purification and Enlightenment.* During this period the elect are challenged to prepare themselves for Baptism and full reception into the Catholic community. Their focus is now on prayer, fasting, and other spiritual disciplines during the days of Lent.

On the Sundays of Lent there are special minor rites and prayers for the elect. Reflection on the Sunday readings, especially from John's gospel, helps them choose Jesus and his kingdom over the way of Satan and darkness. The elect also learn the Christian creed and the Lord's Prayer—the basic summary of Christian beliefs and the prayer of all those who follow Christ. As the elect prepare for initiation, the whole community focuses on praying for and supporting them.

The sacramental rites of initiation are celebrated during the Easter Vigil on Holy Saturday, the night before Easter Sunday. The elect are baptized, confirmed, and receive Eucharist for the first time as full members of the Body of Christ. Baptism includes a litany, the blessing of water, the Baptism itself, clothing in a white garment, and the presentation of a candle lit from the paschal candle. Confirmation includes a calling down of the Holy Spirit, the laying on of hands, and anointing with sacred chrism.

- *Period 4: Mystagogia.* During the weeks or even months following Easter Sunday, the new Catholic Christians meet to reflect on the meaning of the recent events in their lives. They are supported by the community through a deeper study into the mysteries of the faith, those signs of God's love present in the Church's life and in the lives of all Christians.

What is Baptism?
CCC 1214–1228; 1277

The Church baptizes because Christ himself commanded it: "Go, therefore, make disciples of all nations; baptize them in the name of the Father and of the Son and of the Holy Spirit" (Matthew 28:19).

Baptism is a sign of God's love for us. Through Baptism, we enter into the mystery of Christ's death and resurrection. The Church calls us to die to sin and accept a new life of redemption in Jesus. Baptism initiates us into the Body of Christ. It forgives sin and offers us the support of the Christian community as we grow more and more like Christ. Because Baptism seals us with a permanent spiritual character, the sacrament cannot be repeated.

How is Baptism of a child administered?
CCC 1229–1231; 1234–1243; 1250–1252

When parents present their children for Baptism, they profess that they are willing to raise their children with Gospel values. The godparent(s) and fellow parishioners promise to support the parents in their commitment. It is appropriately celebrated at a Sunday liturgy and should always be celebrated in an assembly of Christian believers.

The liturgy begins with a greeting from the ordained minister. The minister then welcomes the child by making the Sign of the Cross on the child's forehead, inviting parents and godparents to do the same. After the Liturgy of the Word, he blesses the baptismal water if it is not already blessed and leads the parents, godparents, and the Christians assembled to profess their faith by renewing their baptismal vows.

The minister pours water on the head of the child (or immerses the child in water) and pronounces the words:

> I baptize you in the name of the Father,
> and of the Son,
> and of the Holy Spirit.

Following Baptism, the child's forehead is anointed with oil, a white garment is placed on the child, and a candle lit from the paschal candle is presented to the child by way of his or her parents and godparents. All assembled recite together the Our Father, after which the celebrant concludes the ceremony by blessing the parents and finally the entire congregation.

What do the symbols of Baptism signify?
CCC 1231–1243

- *Water.* To *baptize* means "to plunge or immerse." Water symbolizes life, cleansing, and death. Baptismal water means the death of an old way of being in the world and rebirth into a new way, with Jesus Christ as one's anchor and constant support. Original sin is washed away, and we inherit eternal life as adopted children of God.

- *Oil.* Anointing with consecrated oil or chrism reminds us that the Lord extends salvation to us and sends the Spirit to protect and strengthen us. The root meaning of *Christ* is "anointed one." The oil of Baptism symbolizes that we have been "Christened." We become the anointed of the Anointed One who heals and strengthens, much as medicinal oil helps to heal a wound.

- *White garment.* In the early Church, Christians put on new white robes as they emerged from the baptismal pool.

Today, by putting on this symbol of purity, festivity, and new identity, the baptized person shows a willingness to live a new life in union with the Lord.

- *Light.* A beautiful part of the baptismal liturgy is the presentation of the light of Christ to the newly baptized. The celebrant lights a candle from the paschal (Easter) candle and presents it to the child. Usually a godparent accepts the candle on behalf of the child. This simple liturgical act challenges all present to be the light of Christ, to live lovingly so others can see Christ working in the world.

- *The Trinitarian Formula.* The Church baptizes us in the name of the Blessed Trinity, Father, Son, and Spirit, thus signifying adoption into the divine family. In the the Rite of Baptism, the celebrant asks for the name of the candidate. Christians usually take the name of a saint. Looking to the saints for inspiration and help reveals our faith in the Communion of Saints.

What happens to the unbaptized?
CCC 1257–1261; 1281; 1283

The Church teaches that some form of Baptism in Jesus Christ is necessary for salvation. Traditionally the Church has taught that there are three forms of Baptism: Baptism by water (through the rite), Baptism by blood (the death of martyrs), and Baptism by desire. Baptism by desire refers to those who were not granted the gift of faith but whose lives show that they would have accepted Jesus if they had the chance.

> Those who die for the faith, those who are catechumens, and all those who, without knowing of the Church but acting under the inspiration of grace,

seek God sincerely and strive to fulfill his will, are
saved even if they have not been baptized.

—*Catechism of the Catholic Church*, 1281

What is Confirmation?
CCC 1285–1292; 1302–1305; 1316–1318

Confirmation is one of the Sacraments of Initiation.
Confirmation brings to completion the making of a Christian. Through a renewal of baptismal promises, laying on
of hands, and anointing with sacred chrism, Confirmation
celebrates the gifts of the Holy Spirit working in the lives of
those receiving the sacrament. It confirms and strengthens
their commitment to the Faith and their discipleship in the
Lord Jesus. When an adult or child who has reached the
age of reason (around seven years old) enters the Church
through Baptism, he or she is immediately confirmed. As
mentioned in the question on RCIA, this usually takes place
during the Easter Vigil on Holy Saturday night. Another
common day on which the Sacrament of Confirmation is celebrated for adults and older children is Pentecost, although
other days can be established as well. Children who are
baptized as infants are usually confirmed some years later.

How is the Rite of Confirmation celebrated?
CCC 1298–1301; 1320–1321

When Confirmation is celebrated apart from Baptism, it
usually takes place during a special Mass to stress its place
in the order of Christian initiation—Baptism, Confirmation,
and Eucharist. After the Liturgy of the Word, the presentation of the candidates, and a short homily or instruction,
the bishop—the ordinary minister of this sacrament—and
the concelebrating priests extend their hands over the candidates as the bishop invokes the outpouring of the Holy

Spirit. In some dioceses, priests are delegated by their bishop to confirm in their own parishes, especially during the Easter Season.

Each candidate comes before the bishop (or presiding priest) who anoints the candidate's forehead with chrism in the shape of a cross. He calls each by name saying, "N., be sealed with the Gift of the Holy Spirit." A greeting of peace and the General Intercessions conclude the rite before Mass continues in the usual way.

The anointing with chrism—the mixture of olive oil and perfume that the bishop consecrates on Holy Thursday—symbolizes that the goodness of the newly confirmed must permeate the world. Oil, a symbol of strength, is also a sign of holiness, of one being specially chosen by God. The anointing with the Sign of the Cross on the forehead stresses how a Christian should resemble Jesus Christ and boldly witness to him.

What are the major effects of Confirmation?
CCC 1302–1305

1. *Confirmation confers and seals the fullness of the Holy Spirit.*

    To be sealed or anointed means to become set apart as belonging to someone or to some particular role. At Confirmation we become official ambassadors of Jesus Christ, empowered by the Holy Spirit, and conformed more perfectly to Christ. Confirmation imprints a permanent spiritual mark and because of this can be received only once.

2. *Confirmation strengthens us to live as Christians.*

    To confirm means "to ratify" and "to strengthen." Confirmation perfects the graces of Baptism and grounds us more deeply in our identity as God's children. Confirmation is often celebrated by adolescents on their way to adulthood and in, those instances, can be thought of as a sacrament of maturity. The Lord calls all of us to courageously witness to Christ, and it is this calling that Confirmation affirms and strengthens.

3. *Confirmation deepens the power of the gifts received in Baptism.*

   The Holy Spirit endows us with gifts that strengthen us and enable us to do Christ's work.

14

The Eucharist

The Eucharist is the central act of worship in the Catholic Church. The celebration of Mass is the best expression of our relationship with God the Father, through the saving activity of his Son, in the power of the Spirit. The word *Eucharist* comes from a Greek term meaning "thanksgiving." It is the sublime means by which we offer God our praise and gratitude as an assembly of the faithful.

What does the Eucharist represent?
CCC 1328–1332

The Eucharist is an efficacious sign instituted by Jesus Christ. This means that it symbolizes what it brings about and brings about what it symbolizes. Among other things, the Eucharist represents and brings about the following: spiritual life and nourishment; the sacrifice of love that makes us holy; Christian community and unity; the presence of Jesus Christ in the life of the individual and the Church; the paschal mystery, which brings eternal life.

How is the Eucharist a sacred meal?
CCC 1412

The Eucharist is a commemorative meal that recalls the Last Supper, which Jesus celebrated with his closest disciples on the night before he died. A shared meal often has an intimate quality that implies something beyond simply eating takes place there. Those who share the joy of companionship gather and partake of the same food. The word *companionship* means "breaking bread together." A shared meal is a universal symbol of friendship.

Jesus was aware of the deep meaning associated with meals when he instituted the Eucharist at a traditional Jewish Passover. The Passover meal reminded the Jewish people of God's goodness and fidelity in rescuing them from slavery in Egypt. This new "Passover," the one Jesus instituted, calls to mind our ransom from slavery to sin and the power of death.

In the Eucharist, Jesus comes to us as food and drink, both necessary for human survival. The Eucharist becomes for us spiritual food, without which our faith would surely die. The Eucharist foreshadows our spiritual inheritance, the heavenly banquet where we will be united totally with God and with our brothers and sisters who have gone before us.

What does the eucharistic bread symbolize?
CCC 1412

Bread is a symbol of life. In one form or another, it is the basic and sometimes the only food for vast numbers of human beings. The unleavened bread we use at the Eucharist becomes for us the body of the Lord Jesus. In it we encounter the real presence of Christ; we consume Christ in order to become ourselves his presence in the world.

The use of unleavened bread at Mass carries rich meaning. In the context of the Passover meal that Jesus was celebrating with his disciples, unleavened bread was a reminder of the haste with which the Jews had escaped from Egypt in the time of Moses. They didn't have time to let their bread rise. We use unleavened bread to remind us that we too are a pilgrim people. We have not yet arrived at our heavenly kingdom and are utterly dependent on God's help.

What does the eucharistic wine symbolize?
CCC 1412

In many cultures, wine is the ordinary drink at meals. This was true of the ancient Middle East where Jesus celebrated the Last Supper. Wine has a joyous, communal quality. During the Eucharist, wine is consecrated and becomes for us the Blood of Christ. In it we encounter the real presence of Christ and by consuming join ourselves to his sacrifice of love for the sake of the world. Blood in the scriptures is often a sign of life uniting God with his people. Jesus offered his blood as a sign of the new covenant between God and his people.

How is the Eucharist a sacrifice?
CCC 1333–1334

Another key symbol of the Passover meal is the paschal lamb, which the Jews offered as a sacrifice to God. Jesus became the new Lamb, the perfect sacrifice who offered his life for all people. The Passover meal signified the old covenant; Jesus' sacrificial death and resurrection inaugurate the new covenant.

Sacrifice comes from a Latin word that means "to make holy" or "to do something holy." Holiness refers to sharing God's life, being, and love. Only God can make us holy. The purpose of sacrificing to God is to adore God, to acknowledge God as the source of our life and the creator of all. We also sacrifice to atone for our sins, to give thanks for God's goodness, and to petition God for favors.

The altar wonderfully represents both the meal and the sacrificial symbolism of the Eucharist. It is the altar of sacrifice and the table of the Lord. Additionally, it symbolizes Christ himself, present both as the victim offered for our reconciliation and as our heavenly food.

Catholics believe that Jesus himself instituted the Eucharist at the Last Supper. The Eucharist represents Christ's sacrifice on the Cross, the supreme sign of his love for us. Jesus, God's Son, is also the perfect human being, our representative before God. Through him, all humans receive and respond to God's offer of love. Jesus put himself in his Father's hands. Surrendering himself obediently, he gave up his life for all people.

What is the meaning of the eucharistic sacrifice?
CCC 1356–1373; 1409–1410

When we offer the sacrifice of the Mass, we continue to be made holy by accepting and living the example of our brother and Savior, Jesus Christ. His freely accepted death shows us that love is the way to holiness. When we remember, celebrate, and attempt to live his sacrifice—his way of love—we become Christ's presence in the world.

In what sense is the Eucharist the Blessed Sacrament?
CCC 1328–1330

The Eucharist is the heart of Catholic life. It is the source, center, and summit of the whole life of the Church. It is the primary sacrament, the one from which all others come and the one to which the others point. We call this sacrament *blessed*, a biblical word that means "a communication of God's life to us." *Blessed Sacrament* is an apt name for the sacrament that gives us Christ himself.

Why do we call the Eucharist Holy Communion?
CCC 1331–1332

Communion means "union with." Communion with Jesus unites us with God and all other Christians. It gives us power to live loving lives for the Lord. The Church encourages us to receive the food of salvation when we attend Mass. We should do so worthily and with knowledge of what the Eucharist is. Worthy reception means being free from mortal sin and fasting from food and drink for at least an hour before receiving Communion (except for water and medicine).

When we receive Christ in the Eucharist, we become one with the Lord Jesus. His life enters us and transforms us. Communion with Christ preserves, increases, and renews baptismal graces. It strengthens us spiritually, forgives venial sin, and helps preserve us from future mortal sin.

Receiving Christ in Holy Communion also enables us to recognize Christ in the poorest of his brothers and sisters and unites us more closely to our Christian brothers and sisters. We receive the Body of Christ to become the Body of Christ. As the sign and cause of unity, the Eucharist impels us to unity with all Christians. Receiving the Lord also enables us to share in the spiritual riches of all those heroic Christians who have gone before us.

What is meant by the Real Presence?
CCC 1374–1381; 1413; 1418

Catholics believe that Jesus is truly present in the community assembled for worship. We also believe that he is present in the priest who presides over the Eucharist in Christ's name, and in the proclamation of the Word of God. Lastly, we believe that Jesus is most especially present in the sacred species of bread and wine.

Exactly how Jesus is present in Holy Communion is of course a fundamental mystery of the faith, a mystery on which the faithful continue to contemplate. The Church uses the word *transubstantiation* to express that at the consecration of the Mass the substances of the bread and wine change into the substance of Jesus. By this we do not mean the physical presence of the historical person Jesus of Nazareth, but a far more profound reality—the Risen Christ, his glorified body and blood, the very essence of the second person of the Trinity. To receive the Real Presence in the consecrated bread or in the consecrated wine is to receive Christ in his fullness, since he is fully present in both.

Our Lord's presence endures in the sacred species of the Blessed Sacrament. In Catholic churches the Blessed Sacrament is reserved in a tabernacle, a sacred box or container usually located in a chapel set aside for eucharistic adoration or at a side altar. Eucharistic adoration is a type of devotional prayer in which many Catholics find great spiritual nourishment. It involves prayer and contemplation in the presence of the reserved Blessed Sacrament.

What does the word Mass mean?
CCC 1232

The term *Mass* is derived from the Latin words recited at the dismissal, *"Ite missa est,"* which mean "Go, you are sent." This reminds us of our duty to love and serve the Lord in all the people we meet. When we "break bread" in the name of Jesus, we are celebrating our communion with one another and receiving the source of our life, the Lord Jesus. In this sacred meal, he reminds us to take him out into the world, a world that desperately needs his love.

How is the Eucharist a ritual?
CCC 1099; 1324–1327

Like all liturgy, the Mass is a religious ritual. It is a renewal of the new covenant in Jesus Christ, which enables us to enter into the events we celebrate. The ritual of the Eucharist is a patterned memorial of the events Jesus enacted for our salvation. This memorial does three things:

(1) It celebrates, recalls, and commemorates the past of our salvation—the life, death, and resurrection of Jesus; (2) it celebrates the paschal mystery as it unfolds in our present; and (3) it looks to the future of the Church and life with the Lord at the eternal banquet of heaven.

What are the parts of the Mass?
CCC 1345–1355; 1408

The Mass consists of Introductory Rites, the Liturgy of the Word, the Liturgy of the Eucharist, and Concluding Rite. In the Liturgy of the Word we hear the Word of God proclaimed in the scripture readings and derive nourishment from it. We are challenged to make it part of our lives and to respond to it. In the Liturgy of the Eucharist we do precisely that by offering praise and thanksgiving to God for the life, death, and resurrection of Jesus. We fully participate in the Eucharist when we receive the Lord in Holy Communion.

Introductory Rites

- *Entrance:* The Mass begins with a procession accompanied with an appropriate hymn.

- *Greeting:* The priest and people make the Sign of the Cross. The priest greets the people, and they respond.

- *Penitential Act:* The priest and people acknowledge their sinfulness and ask God's forgiveness.

- *Gloria*: This great hymn of praise is sung, acknowledging God's goodness.

- *Collect:* The priest offers a prayer that draws members of the community into a spiritual unity and helps prepare them for worship.

Liturgy of the Word

- *Readings:* The first reading is usually from the Old Testament, the second from the latter part of the New Testament, the third from one of the gospels. Psalm verses are recited between the readings, and alleluias are sung before the Gospel.

- *Homily:* The celebrant or deacon relates the readings to everyday life.

- *Profession of Faith:* Together the people acknowledge their common beliefs.

- *Prayer of the Faithful:* The community's petitions for the needs of the Church, the world, public authorities, individuals, and the local community are presented.

Liturgy of the Eucharist

- *Preparation of the Altar and Gifts:* The gifts of bread and wine are brought forward in procession, the altar is prepared, and a prayer is said over the gifts.

- *Eucharistic Prayer:* The Eucharistic Prayer includes the words Jesus said at the Last Supper, the Memorial Acclamation, and concludes with the Doxology or prayer in praise of the Trinity. There are several Eucharistic Prayers that are used for various occasions.

- *Communion Rite:* This part of the Mass includes the Lord's Prayer, the prayer for deliverance, the prayer for peace (after which a sign of peace is exchanged), and the Breaking of the Bread while the "Lamb of God" is sung or recited. After the reception of Communion, the priest offers a prayer of petition on behalf of the community.

- *Concluding Rite:* The Mass is brought to a close with a Solemn Final Blessing and a dismissal that sends the assembly forth to continue the work of the Gospel.

What is the Sunday obligation?
CCC 1382–1390; 1415; 1417

In the early Church, celebrating the Eucharist was commonly understood to be a great privilege and an essential part of being a Christian. But over time, the Church had to pass a law reminding Catholics of their obligation to worship the Lord weekly in the Eucharist. Weekly attendance at Sunday or Saturday evening Mass is once again understood as foundational to Catholic life. Going to Mass, even when it is difficult to do so or when we simply do not feel like going, shows love for God and our fellow pilgrims. We share ourselves and publicly proclaim that we want to worship and thank God for all good gifts, especially our salvation through his Son, Jesus.

Recall the meaning of liturgy as "the people's work." Jesus himself tells us that to be his followers, we must walk the extra mile, stand out, and be different. The Christian life is also a communal life; we need the help, encouragement, and love of others. Above all, we need the Lord. We need the Word of God to nourish and challenge us. We need the Eucharistic Lord himself to transform us and make us like himself.

15

Sacraments of Healing:
Penance and Anointing of the Sick

We all sin, and when we do, our spiritual health suffers. We become alienated from God, others, and even our true selves. At other times we are not physically well. Our bodies are sick with diseases, the frailties of old age, or severe injuries. Our Lord Jesus left with us two powerful signs of his love to assist us at times like these. He knows both our spiritual and physical sicknesses, and he has come to restore us to health. The Lord continues his work of healing today in the Sacraments of Penance and the Anointing of the Sick.

What is the scriptural basis for the Sacrament of Penance?
CCC 1440–1445

Jesus came to forgive sin and to heal the wounded relationships that sin causes. He empowered his Church to continue his ministry of healing, forgiving, and reconciling when he commanded his disciples to forgive sin in his name:

> Receive the Holy Spirit.
> If you forgive anyone's sins, they are forgiven;
> if you retain anyone's sins, they are retained.

> —John 20:23

What are the traditional names for this sacrament?
CCC 1422–1429; 1486

This sacrament is usually known as the Sacrament of Penance or Reconciliation. Quite commonly it is simply called *Confession*, since in it we confess our sins. We call it

Penance (a word meaning "conversion") because it is an aid in the process of repentance, which begins with sorrow for sin, and moves to outward acknowledgment of that sin, the making of amends, and the letting go of that sin. *Reconciliation* means "coming back together." This term emphasizes our need to repair the harmed relationships with God and others that our sins have caused. *Confession* bears a twofold meaning in the celebration of the forgiveness of our sins. We both confess (admit) our sinfulness and confess (state that we believe in) the healing power of God's mercy.

What are the key elements of the Sacrament of Penance?
CCC 1450–1460

The Sacrament of Penance involves three acts of the penitent—contrition, confession, and satisfaction (penance)—as well as the words of absolution announced by the priest. An important preliminary step to take before approaching the sacrament of Penance is a good examination of conscience in which the Holy Spirit helps us uncover areas of sinfulness in our lives. Reflecting on key biblical texts such as the Sermon on the Mount or the Ten Commandments is a good place to begin.

What is contrition?
CCC 1451–1454

Contrition is "heartfelt sorrow and aversion for the sin committed along with the intention of sinning no more" (*Decree on Penance*, 6). Contrition is the heart of conversion, which brings us back to God who is our loving, forgiving Father. Contrition enables us to approach the sacrament with the joy and expectation of God's own child.

Why "confess" our sins?
CCC 1455–1458

Confession is an external sign of interior sorrow. Through it, we meet the Christian community in the person of the priest and face our own sinful condition in the eyes of God. Confession also forces sin out into the open, thus emphasizing its social nature. We should always confess our sins while keeping in mind God's loving mercy.

The Church requires us to confess the serious sins of which we are aware by number and kind at least once a year. The Sacrament of Penance is the sole, ordinary means for Catholics conscious of mortal sin to be reconciled with God and the Church. In this sacrament, Christ tells each person individually: "I forgive you. Go in peace."

The Church does not strictly require the confession of venial sins. But we should use this sacrament for venial sins because sacramental confession heightens our sense of sin, conforms us to Christ, and puts us in touch with the Holy Spirit who calls us to holiness. And frequent recourse to this sacrament helps us uproot sin from our lives by the opportunity to receive guidance from the priest to whom we confess our sins.

What is the value of doing an act of penance?
CCC 1468–1570

If we have true conversion, we want to make up for our sins, amend our lives, and repair any injuries we have caused. The priest assigns a penance (satisfaction) to help us correct the harm done or to serve as a spiritual remedy for our sins. We should accept and joyfully perform these acts of satisfaction, such as prayers, good works, or directly seeking to reconcile a harmed relationship.

What is absolution?
CCC 1449

The priest serves as the Lord's representative and announces the words of absolution on behalf of the Church. When the priest holds his hands over the penitent's head and recites the words, "I absolve you from your sins in the name of the Father, and of the Son, and of the Holy Spirit," Christ himself is giving us the sign we as humans need to know that we are forgiven.

What is a Christian conscience?
CCC 1776–1782; 1795–1797

Conscience is a practical judgment concerning whether "human acts are in conformity or not with the law of God written on the heart" (*The Splendor of Truth,* 59). It is a judgment that helps us know what we must do or not do: to love and do good and to avoid evil. The judgment of conscience also assesses acts already performed. There are two key principles to keep in mind when dealing with judging right and wrong. First, we must properly form our consciences. Second, we must follow our consciences.

How do we properly form our consciences?
CCC 1783–1789; 1798; 1802

The duty to obey one's conscience underscores the necessity of properly forming it. All of us make mistakes, and at times all of us simply do not choose what is good. Ignorance, simply not knowing the right thing to do or the wrong thing to avoid, can cause us to make false judgments. Emotions can cloud our consciences, tempting us to do things simply because they feel good. Conformity to what others are doing can also muddy our decisions. Taking care in developing a strong conscience is necessary to leading a moral life.

Steps to Forming a Good Conscience

1. *Find the facts.* What is the issue? Who is involved? Where? When? How?

2. *Examine your motives.* Why do you want to do this?

3. *Think of the possible effects.* How will this action (or non action) affect you, others, society as a whole? What if everyone did this?

4. *Consider alternatives.* Is there another way to act?

5. *What does the law have to say?* Consider both laws of the Church and society's laws. The law is not opposed to conscience. As a matter of fact, it greatly helps to form it. One way to understand law is that it is the end result of or an articulation of a group's understanding of right and wrong (the group's conscience).

6. *What is the reasonable thing to do?* Because we are people with minds, we must use them in figuring out the right thing to do. Ask yourself what the reasonable decision is.

7. *What does your own experience and that of other people say about the issue?*

8. *What would Jesus have done?* How does this action measure up to Jesus' yardstick of love? What does the New Testament have to say? Jesus is the one perfect human response to God. Seek out his will and his example before making a decision.

9. *What is the teaching of the Church?* Sincere Catholics consider it a serious obligation to consult and follow magisterial teaching on moral issues as well as to learn from competent theologians and other teachers in the Church. There is a wealth of moral teaching beyond what is

explicitly expressed in the written laws of the Church that can help you clarify matters of conscience.

10. *Pray for guidance.* The Lord will help you if you ask.

11. *Admit that you sometimes sin and might be wrong.*

12. *Follow your conscience.* It is always wrong to act contrary to a well-formed conscience.

What is sin?
CCC 1846–1853; 1870–1873

Sin is a failure to love ourselves, others, and God. It is a breakdown in covenant love. Without a healthy concept of sin, people tend to see little need for Jesus, the one who frees us from sin. We talk of sin to stress our conviction that God forgives us and in the person of Jesus has rescued us from its effects.

What is original sin?
CCC 190; 197; 416–417

Original sin refers to that condition of disharmony into which all humans are born. Universal human experience would seem to confirm the Catholic teaching that we are born into a sinful state—that is, a frail state of being—that if left unremedied will lead to personal sin. Baptism remedies the situation by joining us to Christ and to his Church so that we might be reconciled with God.

What is personal sin?
CCC 1854

Personal or actual sin is any free and deliberate action, word, thought, or desire that turns us away from God's law of love. It can be seen as a weakening or killing of our loving relationship with the Father. Sin breaches our baptismal mission to advance God's reign in this world, an obligation we have to God and to one another.

What is venial sin?
CCC 1862–1866; 1875–1876

Traditionally, venial sin refers to those acts and attitudes that fail to help us grow in our loving relationship with God or that weaken that relationship. Our goal is total union with God; our direction should be one of growing closer to God each day. Venial sin involves less serious matters than mortal sin, or happens when a person does not fully reflect on or consent to what he or she is doing. All sin has social consequences; there are always other people affected by what we do.

What is mortal sin?
CCC 1855–1861; 1874

Mortal sin is the harboring of a serious attitude or the commission of some serious action that kills the relationship of love between God and the sinner. In mortal sin, a person freely and consciously rejects God, God's law, and the covenant of love that God offers, preferring oneself or some created reality that is contrary to God's will.

There are three conditions that must be met before a person sins mortally. First, the action or attitude itself must involve grave matter—for example, murder, apostasy, or adultery. Second, the person must be fully aware that what he or she is doing is sinful. We are not guilty of mortal sin for doing something we truly do not know is wrong. The third condition for mortal sin is that the person must deliberately consent to the evil. Modern psychology tells us there are a number of forces and drives that limit our freedom; however, humans do have some freedom and are capable of serious and deliberate wrongdoing. Our obligation is to avoid those situations that might limit our freedom and keep us from doing the right thing.

What is the role of reconciliation?
CCC 1468–1470; 1496

Traditionally, we speak of a person who has turned completely away from God's love and is no longer in relationship with God as being in "the state of mortal sin." To correct this situation the sinner must repent—that is, turn back to God, admit his or her wrongdoing, and acknowledge the need for forgiveness.

Catholics celebrate the Sacrament of Reconciliation in which God's forgiveness and healing love are given to us. The point of Jesus' parable of the Prodigal Son (Luke 15:11–31) is that no matter what we do or how often we do it, God's love is always there for us. We need only repent—that is, turn to God and accept his love. In essence, Christian morality is saying yes to God's love, letting it shine on us, and then living a life of light that shines out to others.

What is the scriptural basis for the Sacrament of the Anointing of the Sick?
CCC 1499–1510; 1526

Jesus Christ is a healer. Jesus saw the hurting people in his midst and responded to them holistically—both to their bodies and spirits. Healing was a principal sign of the coming of God's kingdom. Jesus' healing ministry should be seen in the context of his forgiving sin and his proclamation of God's kingdom and the need for repentance.

Jesus charged his disciples to continue his message and mission. Thus, the early Church celebrated and proclaimed the Good News of salvation by continuing Jesus' healing ministry. The Letter of James provides the scriptural basis for the Sacrament of Anointing, the symbol of love:

> Any one of you who is ill should send for the elders of the Church, and they must anoint the sick person with oil in the name of the Lord and pray over him. The prayer of faith will save the sick person and the Lord will raise him up again; and if he has committed any sins, he will be forgiven. So confess your sins to one another, and pray for one another to be cured.
>
> —James 5:14–16

How is the Sacrament of the Anointing of the Sick celebrated?
CCC 1517–1519

Today, the sacrament is administered not only to the dying but also to those who are sick. The celebration of this sacrament attempts to include the prayerful support of the Christian community (the family, friends, and parish community of the sick person). It reintroduces the laying on of hands, a biblical symbol of Jesus' touch and of the outpouring of the Spirit of strength, love, and forgiveness.

The rite underscores the need for the sick person to overcome the alienation caused by sickness and suffering. Today's rite also urges the person to assume a more active role, by requesting the sacrament himself or herself rather than having someone else do it. In this sense, Anointing of the Sick is related to the Christian vocation of witnessing; that is, the sick person witnesses to the rest of the community his or her total dependence on God's love and support.

What are the effects of the Anointing of the Sick?
CCC 1520–1523; 1527; 1532

Pain and suffering can make us miserable and weaken our faith in a loving, caring God. Through this sacrament, the Lord, acting through the Christian community, assures us of his care and concern. He extends his forgiveness and strengthens the sick person through spiritual healing and, at times, physical healing. Through this sacrament, the Lord invites us to integrate our sickness, even a mortal one, into the mystery of his own suffering, death, and resurrection—the paschal mystery that has won for us eternal salvation. The sacrament reminds the community, too, that it must stand by and love its Christian brothers and sisters in times of need.

How is the Anointing of the Sick celebrated?
CCC 1513; 1517–1519; 1524–1525

Typically the Sacrament of the Anointing of the Sick is celebrated individually during a serious illness or before a serious operation. If possible, family and friends should be present. There is a growing trend toward celebration of the sacrament within the context of the Eucharist.

The rite itself begins with a greeting, a sprinkling with holy water, a penitential rite, and the Liturgy of the Word, which recalls the Lord's healing power. All present then join in a litany of prayers for the sick. After the priest lays his hands on the person to be anointed, he blesses the oil and then anoints the forehead and hands. He prays:

> Through this holy anointing may the Lord in his love and mercy help you with the grace of the Holy Spirit. Amen. May the Lord who frees you from sin save you and raise you up.
>
> Amen.

A prayer after the anointing and the Lord's Prayer follow. Holy Communion may then be given before the final blessing, which concludes the liturgy.

16

Christian Marriage

A ll sacraments are signs of God's friendship and love; they are celebrations of his ongoing presence to us in our ordinary lives. Christian marriage, celebrated in the Sacrament of Matrimony, is truly the sacrament of friendship. Christians who marry in the Lord are a living sign of God's love in human relationships, in friendship, in life-giving procreation, in family living.

What is the Sacrament of Marriage?
CCC 1601; 1660

In the Sacrament of Matrimony a baptized man and woman vow their love in an exclusive, permanent, sexual partnership. This union is marked by love, respect, care and concern, and a commitment to share responsibility in the raising of a family if God should bless them with children.

Christian marriage is an extraordinary sign of God working through and in the ordinary. A good marriage is a holy covenant involving three persons. The couple is joined on their life's journey by Jesus Christ who promises to bless, sustain, and rejoice in their union.

In the covenant of Christian marriage, a husband and wife freely bind themselves together for life. Theirs is a commitment to love exclusively.

What does the Old Testament reveal about marriage?
CCC 1602–1608

In the book of Genesis, God revealed to the Jewish people two profound truths about the purposes of marriage. First, marriage is a share in God's creative act of bringing new life into the world. Second, marriage is meant to enhance, celebrate, and increase the love between wife and husband. Genesis tells us that God established marriage and sex and declared that they are good.

What does the New Testament reveal about marriage?
CCC 1613–1616; 1659

The New Testament reveals further important insights into the nature of marriage. Jesus' attendance at the wedding feast of Cana underscores the goodness of marriage. When Jesus explicitly teaches about marriage, he reaffirms the original intention of his Father—that marriage should be a permanent, exclusive love relationship. "Everyone who divorces his wife and marries another is guilty of adultery, and the man who marries a woman divorced by her husband commits adultery" (Luke 16:18).

The union of a husband and wife is like the union of Christ with his Church. Marriage is a covenant, a total, lifelong commitment that mirrors Christ's love for his Church.

What is the proximate preparation for a Christian marriage?
CCC 1632–1637

Preparation for a Christian marriage in most dioceses includes a policy that the engaged couple attends premarriage conferences. These Church-sponsored classes give the couple an opportunity to learn about the sacramental commitment of marriage and learn about many practicalities of married life from married couples. At times experts in natural family planning or family communications also speak with the couples. Topics examined include love and communication, the raising of a family, the role of a faith life in marriage, and plans for the actual ceremony.

What are the requirements for a valid marriage?
CCC 1625–1631; 1662

To celebrate the Sacrament of Marriage validly, the couple must be of mature age, unmarried, not closely related by blood or marriage, and must freely desire to marry. They must intend to commit themselves to a lifelong covenant of love. Furthermore, they must be capable of sharing sexually, since sexual intercourse is a sign of mutual love and union, the full expression of the mutual love between husband and wife. Finally, the couple must be open to the possibility of raising a family if God blesses the marriage with children.

How is the Sacrament of Marriage celebrated?
CCC 1621–1624; 1663

Ordinarily, Christian marriage takes place during Mass if both partners are Catholic. The spouses, ministers of Christ's grace, confer the Sacrament of Marriage on each other. They express their consent—the indispensable element that brings marriage into being—by exchanging vows in the presence of the priest, two witnesses, and the assembled Christian community. As the Church's official witness, the priest blesses the rings and asks the couple to exchange them as symbols of fidelity and unending love.

The celebration of the wedding ceremony is only one important element in the sacrament. The Sacrament of Marriage unfolds over the years as the husband and wife live out their mutual relationship with each other and the Lord. The risen Lord promises to be with the couple to sustain them on their life journey.

> The Sacrament of Matrimony gives spouses the grace to love each other with the love with which Christ has loved his Church; the grace of the sacrament thus perfects the human love of the spouses,

strengthens their indissoluble unity and sanctifies
them on the way to eternal life.

> —*Catechism of the Catholic Church*, 1661

Why is Christian marriage forever?
CCC 1646–1651; 1665

Christian marriage is a permanent commitment because
it is a prime way to bring Christ into the world and pass on
the Christian faith. This is certainly true for the children who
result from marriage. They need the stable, reassuring love
of a solid marriage to develop healthy attitudes toward life
and toward God.

But a faithful marriage is a powerful sign to others as
well. The Christian husband and wife point to the mystery
of God's love at work in ordinary life. Their fidelity and
exclusive love are extraordinary signs to the world of God's
fidelity and undying love for his people.

Jesus himself underscored the permanence of the marriage bond:

> Have you not read that the Creator from the begin-
> ning made them male and female and that he said:
> This is why a man leaves his father and mother and
> becomes attached to his wife, and the two become
> one flesh? They are no longer two, therefore, but
> one flesh. So then, what God has united, human
> beings must not divide.

> —Matthew 19:4–6

The covenant made between two validly married Catholics can only be dissolved by the death of one of the partners. In extraordinary circumstances, a couple may separate
for the good of the children and the individuals involved.
Though the civil authority may dissolve the legal aspects of

a valid marriage (called in civil law a divorce), the state has no authority to dissolve a true Christian marriage.

Christ calls his disciples to high standards. The Church encourages a person who is suffering from a broken marriage to continue to celebrate the sacraments and remain close to the Christian community. The Lord promises in a special way to bless those who suffer most. Fellow Christians should support hurting brothers and sisters and pray for them.

What is an annulment?
CCC 1629

An annulment is an official declaration of the Church that what appeared to be a valid Christian marriage in fact was not. A couple may have been psychologically immature when they entered the marriage, or lacked true understanding of the demands a marriage covenant makes. One or both partners might not have given free, true consent to the marriage. Perhaps one or both partners never intended to have children or are incapable of sexual relations.

A "failed" marriage may never have been a true Christian marriage to begin with. In these cases, the couple should submit their situation to the diocesan marriage tribunal (court) for examination and judgment. If it can be shown that the marriage was not valid from the beginning, then the individuals involved are free to enter a true Christian marriage in the future.

What does the Church teach about sexual sharing?
CCC 2360–2365; 2397

The Catholic community praises married love as a great gift from God. Sexual intercourse is a profound means of love and commitment between a man and a woman. Its purpose in God's plan is twofold: *unitive*—that is, to bond a man and woman together as partners for life; and *procreative*—that is, to share in God's creative activity of bringing new life into the world.

As a deep symbol of love between a man and a woman, sexual intercourse (and all acts leading up to it) expresses a total, unreserved commitment of love. The Church believes this can take place only when a couple has declared lifelong devotion to each other—that is, in a marriage.

What does the Church teach about adultery?
CCC 2380–2381; 2400

Sexual intimacy signifies a total giving and a total receiving. To engage in sexual relations outside of marriage is to misuse this profound sign of human love. Thus adultery—sexual intimacy engaged in by a married person with another who is not his or her spouse—is a serious breach in the covenant love of Christian marriage. Adultery is a failure to honor the fundamental commitment of marriage; it threatens the very stability of the family.

What does the Church teach about fornication?
CCC 2353

Fornication is sexual intercourse engaged in by unmarried people. It is also wrong, because it often exploits others or is indulged in for selfish motives under the guise of love. God intended intimate sexual sharing to express total love and commitment; that kind of love and commitment exists only within the context of marriage.

What does the Church teach about masturbation?
CCC 2352

The Church also teaches that masturbation—self-induced sexual pleasure—is wrong, because it misuses the powers of sex, which in God's plan are directed to sexual intimacy with another and with bringing new life into the world.

What does the Church teach about homosexuality?
CCC 2357–2359

The Church distinguishes between a homosexual condition and homosexual acts. Homosexuality as a condition exists when a person's sexual desires are directed to a member of the same sex rather than to a member of the opposite sex. People with homosexual tendencies do not choose their homosexual condition. They deserve respect, compassion, and sensitivity. Unjust discrimination toward them is un-Christian. However, the Church teaches that homosexual acts are intrinsically disordered and against the natural law. They are a serious violation of God's plan for male/female bonding and are not open to the procreation of life. They can never be approved.

What does the Church teach about family planning?
CCC 2366–2369; 2398

Birth control refers to a couple's deliberate limitation of the number of children they will bring into the world. Christian parents are called upon to plan the size of their families in a responsible way. Physical and psychological health, family finances and overall well being along with civic and global concerns are some of the factors that will help a husband and wife determine the size of their family. The Church teaches that for legitimate reasons a Catholic couple has the right and duty to practice natural methods of birth control.

What is natural birth control?
CCC 2369–2370

Periodic abstinence from sexual relations and natural family planning methods are moral means of birth control because they work in harmony with normal, natural bodily functions. The office of family life or ministry in most dioceses sponsors classes to help train couples in these methods.

What does the Church teach about artificial birth control?
CCC 2370; 2399

Church teaching holds that artificial means of contraception are contrary to God's will. This teaching rests on the Catholic view that marriage is directed to two aims simultaneously: the procreation (and rearing) of children, and the mutual love and affection of the couple. Official Church teaching maintains that any artificial means used to frustrate the natural processes of procreation goes against the very nature of marriage.

In striving to live the ideal, sometimes people fall short. The bishops advise us not to judge the consciences of those couples who fall short of the Church's teaching. This moral judgment is God's to make. Couples must follow their consciences in this and all moral issues, but are obligated to develop well-informed consciences.

17

Christian Ministry: Holy Orders and Service

Disciples learn from and strive to imitate their masters. Christian disciples strive to be like Christ Jesus by loving and serving others in imitation of him.

What is ministry?
CCC 1533, 1544–1545

The common vocation of all Christians is to minister—that is, to serve others in the name of Christ. Minister means "one who serves." Christian ministry means serving others in Christ and because of Christ. Through Baptism, Confirmation, and Eucharist every member of the Church is called to serve others in imitation of Jesus. This is the universal vocation of all disciples. Jesus empowers us for ministry by sending us the Holy Spirit who showers on us the gifts necessary to do God's work.

What are some ways to minister?
CCC 893; 901–903; 941

Ministry involves many different ways to serve others. The obligation of every baptized Christian is to bring Christian values to everyday life. In his social justice teachings, Pope John Paul II reminded all Christians of their need to live in solidarity with the poor. The laity have a preeminent role in serving the cause of peace and justice in the particulars of their own life situations.

In addition to serving in the world, Catholics can serve fellow members of the Church in many ways. The following list includes some of the key opportunities for ministry that the Church encourages the lay faithful to undertake:

- Religious educators, catechists, and teachers
- Eucharistic ministers, lectors, music and art ministers, hospitality ministers
- Ministers to the sick, homebound, and disabled
- Parish councilors and financial consultants
- Ministers to the separated and divorced
- Ministers to the poor

What is the ordained ministry?
CCC 874–879

Ordained ministers serve in one of the structured ministries of the Church; they are entrusted with leading the Church through a special ministry of service to the Christian community and by extension to the whole world. Ordained ministers include bishops, presbyters (priests), and deacons. Their special role is to proclaim God's Word to all people, to lead the Christian community in worship, and to model in a special way the universal Christian vocation of service.

What is the Sacrament of Holy Orders?
CCC 1536–1538; 1548–1553; 1591–1592

Holy Orders can be described as the sacrament of Christian ministry. Through the laying on of hands by a presiding bishop and a prayer of consecration, the Sacrament of Holy Orders confers on certain men a special role of service within the Christian community. Holy Orders deepens the life of Jesus in these men called to serve him and his Church. The sacrament also gives actual graces—divine help—to provide the wisdom and fortitude necessary to live the life of ordained ministers. Finally, the Church teaches that Holy Orders, like Baptism and Confirmation, imparts a sacramental "character" that permanently marks the ordained as a deacon, priest, or bishop—a living sign who points to the Lord and his coming.

What is the role of ministerial priesthood today?
CCC 1546–1547

Ministerial priesthood is often seen in terms of the images of priest, prophet, and king—roles fulfilled by Jesus. Ordained ministers have the special vocation to build up and lead the priestly people in worship (priest), proclaim God's Word (prophet), and imitate Christ's merciful life of service by serving God's people and acting as a sign of Christ in the world (king).

> The ministerial priesthood has the task not only of representing Christ—Head of the Church—before the assembly of the faithful, but also of acting in the name of the whole Church when presenting to God the prayer of the Church, and above all when offering the Eucharistic sacrifice.

> —*Catechism of the Catholic Church*, 1552

What are the functions of bishops, priests, and deacons?
CCC 1554–1571; 1594

Bishop, priest, and deacon are the three ordained ministries of the Church. We speak of bishops as successors of the apostles. The local bishop (known as the "ordinary" of a diocese) is the overseer of the local Church community and a symbol of Church unity. His consecration confers on him the fullness of the Sacrament of Holy Orders: the offices of teaching, governing, and sanctifying. The chief responsibilities of bishops are to preach the Gospel, to see to the administration of the sacraments, and to serve the needy in his diocese. Often the local ordinary or head of a diocese will have auxiliary bishops to assist him in carrying out his role.

Bishops ordain priests to help them carry out their duties of preaching the Gospel, shepherding the faithful, and celebrating divine worship. Deacons cooperate with the bishop and priests in liturgical celebrations, in the distribution of Communion, in preaching the Gospel, in baptizing, in witnessing and blessing marriages, in presiding at some of the funeral rites, and in the social outreach of the Church.

How is Holy Orders celebrated?
CCC 1572–1574; 1597

The Sacrament of Holy Orders is celebrated in three forms, one for the ordination of a bishop, another for the ordination of a priest, the third for the ordination of a deacon. The three forms of the rite are quite similar. Ordination is usually celebrated within Mass presided over by a bishop or bishops. God's people, from whom an ordained minister is called in order to serve the Christian community and all people everywhere, are present at this celebration.

At the ordination of priests, candidates are called forth by name after the Liturgy of the Word. The bishop questions them about their willingness to share in his care for God's people—in celebrating the sacraments, in preaching God's Word, and in a life dedicated to God's reign. The visible sign of ordination is the laying on of hands by the bishop who recites a prayer of consecration asking God for the outpouring of the Holy Spirit and gifts for the priestly ministry.

The hands of the newly ordained priests are anointed, and the symbols of their office are conferred (vestments, a chalice containing water and wine, and a paten on which rests the bread to be consecrated). The sign of peace is exchanged. The liturgy continues with the newly ordained concelebrating with the bishop and their fellow priests.

What are the reasons for a celibate clergy?
CCC 1579–1150; 1599

Church law requires priests and bishops of the Roman Catholic Church not to marry. This is known as celibacy. Priests undertake this discipline freely to express their wholehearted commitment to serving both God and his people.

> Called to consecrate themselves with undivided heart to the Lord and to "the affairs of the Lord," they give themselves entirely to God and to men. Celibacy is a sign of this new life to the service of which the Church's minister is consecrated; accepted with a joyous heart celibacy radiantly proclaims the Reign of God.
>
> —*Catechism of the Catholic Church*, 1579

What is a religious vocation?
CCC 914–933

Vocation means "calling," an invitation by the Lord to a special kind of service. One can be called to serve God as a married person, in the single life, as a priest, or in religious life. For most of Christian history, some men (religious brothers or priests belonging to a religious community) and women (religious sisters or nuns) have consecrated themselves to God and the work of God's kingdom by taking vows of poverty, chastity, and obedience.

By taking the vow of poverty, those living the religious life are attempting to free themselves of the things of this world so that they can be attached to the One who is really important, Jesus Christ. By vowing chastity for the sake of the Gospel, religious become a sign to the world that they belong simultaneously to Christ and to all people. Through the vow of obedience, religious commit themselves to serve their religious community, which in turn is dedicated to serving the Christian community. All three vows are positive ways to liberate those living them to a more active life of prayer and service in God's Church.

18

Prayer

We who follow the Lord are called to holiness—that is, to true union with God in both mind and heart. Growth in holiness is a gift from God. The Holy Spirit never forces God's love on us but empowers us to respond freely to the opportunities God gives us. Prayer is an essential way to get closer to God. Catholic tradition offers many different ways to pray, many different paths to our Lord.

What is prayer?
CCC 2558–2567; 2590

A traditional Catholic definition of prayer is "the lifting of one's mind and heart to God." A popular description states that prayer is "loving conversation with God." The great spiritual writer Thomas Merton defined prayer as "the consciousness of one's union with God, an awareness of one's inner self." However we define prayer, it always begins with turning to God and becoming aware of God's presence. When we pray, we seek the marvelous activity of God in our lives.

In the public prayer of the Church, Catholics come and pray together as members of Christ's family to praise God, seek forgiveness, ask for help, or offer thanks. Private prayer, on the other hand, is engaged in by an individual Christian in personal communication with God. Private prayer can certainly be for others; we can and should pray for our families, friends, and members of the Church, for leaders, for people in need, for our enemies, indeed for all people.

When we recite the Hail Mary or read the psalms aloud, we are engaging in formal vocal prayer; we are using prayers already composed according to a certain form. But we are not limited to saying formal prayers. Our prayer can also be spontaneous—that is, in our own words and following no set formula.

What are the purposes of prayer?
CCC 2623–2643

One way to distinguish among the different kinds of prayer is through the acronym ACTS, which helps us remember the four purposes of prayer: adoration, contrition, thanksgiving, and supplication. We pray to adore God as the source of all blessings and to praise God as gracious, loving, and saving. We express sorrow to God for the sins we have committed when we offer prayers of contrition. We thank God for the many gifts God has given us. Finally, we offer prayers of supplication, or petition. These are requests for God's help. A special form of petition is intercessory prayer, which asks God's help on behalf of other people, a special way to show love and mercy.

What are the basics of prayer?
CCC 2663–2698; 2720; 2757

To grow in friendship with the Lord requires time. It is good to remember the following:

- *Find a place and time.* You can pray anywhere, but it is good to find a special place where you can slow down, relax, and focus your attention. You can also pray at any time, but it is a good idea to select a regular time each day. Prayer is a habit. We learn to pray by praying.

- *Relax.* Prayer demands our attention. Masters of the spiritual life suggest that we assume a body position that keeps us alert but also helps us relax. We should also spend time calming our bodies so that our minds and spirits are free to commune with the Lord.

- *Maintain a good attitude.* Prayer requires openness and devotion to God. It is always good to begin our prayer by recalling God's presence and friendship and the many gifts he has bestowed on us.

How can we develop a positive attitude toward prayer?
CCC 2725–2731; 2734–2737; 2742–2745

Remember that God is *Abba.* Our God is a loving Father. We need never fear approaching him. God knows our needs and is vitally concerned with our lives. We can trust our Father.

- *Be persistent.* Jesus taught that we should "pray continually and never lose heart."

- *Be confident.* Deep faith in God should accompany our persistence in prayer.

- *Be humble.* Jesus instructed his disciples to pray simply and humbly. He also taught us there is no need to speak many words because our heavenly Father already knows our needs. Humility is a true sign of our love for God.

- *Be forgiving.* The God of forgiveness wants us to approach him with forgiveness in our hearts. This is a sign of sincerity and peace that will help make our prayer beneficial.

What is vocal prayer?
CCC 2700–2704

Vocal prayers are usually said aloud and with others—for example, at Mass. They can either follow a prescribed formula or be spontaneous. Vocal prayers can also be "one-liners"—for example, "Holy Spirit, enlighten me" or "Jesus, help me."

Some prayers are so familiar to us that we forget to reflect on what we are saying. To counteract this tendency, it is helpful to pause before praying, recall God's presence and the reason why we are praying, and then consciously reflect on the prayer.

What is special about the Lord's Prayer?
CCC 2759–2865

Jesus, a model pray-er, taught us the Lord's Prayer, which serves as a pattern for Christian prayer. As the Church Father, Tertullian, observed, it summarizes the whole Gospel.

- In the Lord's Prayer we address God as *Abba*, who has adopted us into the divine family and who reveals that we are related to all other humans. We are God's people.

- We acknowledge God's majesty and mysterious presence in heaven and in the hearts of the just.

- We pray that everyone will acknowledge God's holiness, and we commit ourselves to "hallowing" God's name by living in God's love.

- We pray for the full coming of God's reign. In doing so, we join Jesus in his work of spreading God's peace and justice, truth and service, especially to the needy.

- We petition God to give us our daily bread: what we need for physical life—food, shelter, clothing; psychological life—friendship, love, and companionship; and spiritual life—the Eucharist.

- We humbly ask God to forgive us our sins. And we pledge that we will forgive others as we have been forgiven.

- We petition God not to allow us to take the path that leads to sin. We ask God to strengthen us to persevere to the end of our days by avoiding the snares of Satan and an often materialistic, pleasure-driven, and violent society that ignores God and tempts us to rely solely on ourselves.

How do we pray with scripture?

Christians from the earliest centuries have found reading and reflecting on the Bible as the living Word of God a most helpful means of spiritual growth. To read the Bible prayerfully, select a passage, find a quiet place, and recall the presence of God within your heart and in the sacred scriptures. Ask the Lord to help you see that what you are to read is his Word, his self-communication spoken directly to you.

Begin reading slowly and reflectively, pausing frequently to see what the text is saying and what meaning it might have for your life. While reading, turn frequently to the Lord and speak to him as to a friend, asking him to make his Word take root in your life.

After your period of prayer, think back over what you learned and take a key insight with you. Thank the Lord for what he has given you. Then, throughout the day, return to the insight you gained as a way of remembering the Lord's gift to you.

What is meditation?
CCC 2705–2708

The Church has long had a rich tradition of both meditation and contemplation. Meditation is attuning oneself to God, thinking about God and trying to become aware of God's presence in our lives. It usually involves active use of the mind and imagination. There are many methods of meditation. All of them, though, suggest the following:

1. Find a quiet place, a place where you will not be disturbed.

2. Quiet your body. Relax your body so your mind can focus on the meditation.

3. Direct your attention to some object of meditation. You may focus on a crucifix, or recall how the Lord met you through another person. You might also simply focus on a very brief scripture passage.

4. Pause periodically to talk intimately to the Lord.

5. At the end of your prayer time, thank the Lord for his friendship and any spiritual insights he might have given you. Make a resolution to do something with your insights and return to them periodically throughout the day.

What is contemplation?
CCC 2709–2919

Contemplation, sometimes known as "mental prayer," is more concerned about receptivity than is meditation. A person doesn't really try to think about anything. Rather, the pray-er puts himself or herself in God's presence and simply enjoys God's loving company. Contemplation is wordless prayer. Contemplation is a way of praying without images and words in order to meet the living God who transcends human comprehension and understanding.

What is the Jesus Prayer?
CCC 2665–2669

The Jesus Prayer consists of the words, "Lord Jesus Christ, Son of God, have mercy on me, a sinner." Alternative forms are "Jesus, have mercy on me" or, simply, "Jesus." Rhythmic breathing is often used when reciting this prayer.

How does praying affect us?
CCC 2738–2741

Praying on a regular basis keeps our true goal in life before us. It helps us become more aware of God's presence and realize God's deep love for us as individuals. This awareness helps make us more loving, patient, and attuned to what is really important. Prayer creates within us a strong foundation from which to make moral decisions rooted in love and intimate communion with God, who creates and binds all humanity together.

19

The Communion of Saints and the Blessed Mother

The Acts of the Apostles and the New Testament epistles (letters) commonly refer to Christians as "the saints." The claim being made was not that Christians were already perfect but that the Lord calls us to holiness—the word *saint* meaning "holy one." Through our baptismal initiation into Jesus' own life of holiness, Christians have been given a privileged vocation: to become saints in imitation of our Lord.

Who belongs to the Communion of Saints?
CCC 954–955; 962

The Communion of Saints—that is, the communion of the holy—includes all those who are now living on earth (the pilgrim Church), those who are being purified in purgatory (the Church suffering), and those who are blessed in heaven (the Church in glory).

The term *Communion of Saints* also underscores that the People of God, the Church, is a eucharistic community. The Church is a community of people, a real communion, gathered around the eucharistic table of the risen Lord. Through the power of the Holy Spirit, the Church is united into a communion of love and holiness as it partakes of the gift of the risen Lord, the source of all holiness.

What is the basis for belief in the Communion of Saints?
CCC 958–959; 1475

The doctrine of the Communion of Saints flows from our belief that we Christians are closely united in the Spirit of Jesus Christ. The bond of love makes us one. Those of us who are still living depend on the prayers and good works of our Christian brothers and sisters who are united to us in the friendship of the Lord. We also believe in the value of prayer for our departed brothers and sisters who are being purified in purgatory. Finally, we believe that those Christian heroes whom we call saints in heaven are vitally interested in those of us who are still living.

Who is a saint?
CCC 828–957

A saint is a person living in a state of grace. Saints are Christian models of holiness.

Under the guidance of the Holy Spirit the Catholic Church will at times declare in a public and formal way that a person who lived a good life and died a death joined to Jesus is a saint. These are the canonized saints of the Church. The process leading to canonization involves a careful study of that person's life and signs from God (usually miracles performed in that person's name) that this person is truly worthy of imitation by the universal Church.

Why do we pray to the saints?
CCC 955–957

Devotion to the saints is a traditional means to holiness. We do not pray to the saints as though they were God. Rather, we petition them to intercede for us with our heavenly Father. They are living a deep, personal, and loving relationship with God and have proven their friendship by the extraordinary goodness of their lives while on earth. We pray to the saints, especially those to whom we feel particularly close, to befriend us. We ask these personal heroes to take our petitions to God on our behalf.

What is Mary's role in the Church?
CCC 964–968; 973

Mary, foremost among the saints, has a special place in the story of salvation history. The New Testament tells us that she was singled out and graced by God for the special and unique privilege of being the mother of the Savior. As Jesus began his public ministry, Mary faithfully witnessed and supported him. With courage and sorrow in her heart, she stood at the foot of the Cross in Jesus' dying moments. Finally, the Bible tells us that Mary was with the apostles praying in the upper room after Jesus' resurrection, expectantly awaiting the coming of the Holy Spirit. The Church teaches that Mary is the greatest Christian saint of all, the perfect model of Christian faith, the first among disciples.

What are some of Mary's titles?
CCC 969

The Church honors Mary with many titles such as Our Lady, Mother of God, Our Lady of the Immaculate Conception, Blessed Mother, Mother of the Church, Ever Virgin, Queen of Heaven and Earth. These titles reflect what the Church believes and teaches about her.

What do we mean by the Immaculate Conception?
CCC 490–493; 508; 722

The Church teaches that Mary was conceived without original sin. This means that from the first moment of her existence Mary was full of grace—that is, free of any alienation from God caused by original sin. Because of Mary's special role in God's saving plan, she was graced with this divine favor in anticipation of her son's death and resurrection.

What is the Church's teaching about Mary's virginity?
CCC 484–489; 494; 496–499; 502–503; 510; 723

In the Apostles' Creed, we profess that Jesus was conceived by the Holy Spirit and born of the Virgin Mary. Mary conceived Jesus without a human father, and from its earliest centuries, the Church has taught that she remained ever virgin.

How is Mary the Mother of God and the Mother of the Church?
CCC 495; 501; 509; 724–726; 963

At the Council of Ephesus in AD 431, the Church Fathers declared that Mary is *theotokos*—that is, "bearer of God." By being the mother of Jesus, Mary is truly the Mother of God. It is most appropriate for Christians to address Mary with this lofty title. But Mary is also our mother, the Mother of the Church. By giving Mary to us as our mother, the Lord wishes the Church to learn what God does for those he loves. The Church also has a maternal role and can learn much from Mary, the perfect model of faith, obedience, fidelity, compassion, and prayerfulness. Mary is the model of Christian holiness and an image of God's love for his people.

What is the Assumption?
CCC 966; 974

In 1950 Pope Pius XII officially proclaimed the doctrine of the assumption: "The Immaculate Mother of God, the ever Virgin Mary, having completed the course of her earthly life, was assumed body and soul into heavenly glory." In her assumption, Mary was preserved from the decay of death. Mary, the mother of the Savior, has a unique share in the Lord's resurrection.

Why do Catholics have special veneration for Mary?
CCC 970; 972; 975

Catholics venerate Mary because she is the Mother of God and Mother of the Church. By praying to and honoring Mary in a special way, we are led to love her and to imitate her many virtues, especially her total commitment to God's will and her single-hearted faith in God's work.

Sometimes Catholics are accused of worshipping Mary as though she were God. True devotion to Mary honors Mary; God alone may be worshipped. When we pray in Mary's honor, we are really thanking and praising God for blessing one of our sisters.

What is the Rosary?
CCC 971; 2708

The Rosary is a perfect blend of vocal prayers and meditation. The vocal prayers center on the recitation of a number of decades of Hail Marys, each decade introduced by the Lord's Prayer and concluded by a Glory Be. During the recitation of these vocal prayers, we meditate on certain events, or mysteries, from the life of Christ and Mary. The repetition of the Hail Marys helps to keep our minds from distractions as we meditate on the mysteries. These mysteries are divided into four sets or categories: Joyful, Luminous, Sorrowful, and Glorious.

20

Christian Destiny: The Last Things

One seemingly inevitable defeat that stares all humans in the face is death. But the Good News of Christianity is that death does not have the last word; life does. When we die and our bodies fade from this earth, life is not over, but changed. Jesus taught: "I am the resurrection. Anyone who believes in me, even though that person dies, will live, and whoever lives and believes in me will never die" (John 11:25–26).

What does our faith teach us about death and judgment?
CCC 677–679; 1019

As a result of original sin, people must suffer "bodily death, from which they would have been preserved had they not sinned" (*Church in the Modern World*, 18). The book of Ecclesiastes teaches that it is natural to die: "There is a season for everything. . . . A time for giving birth, a time for dying" (3:1–2). To make sense out of death and our own personal future death, we must look to Jesus Christ.

Death is a great mystery. But Christian faith reveals that Jesus Christ, our Savior, has conquered death and wants us to befriend him in this life so that we can live joyfully with him in eternity. This is not only the Good News of the Gospel—this is the greatest news humanity is privileged to know.

In the *Dictionary of the Bible* John McKenzie writes, "For each [person] the 'day of judgment' is the day on which he [she] makes a permanent decision to accept Jesus Christ or to reject him." This is known as the *particular judgment.* But McKenzie also notes that the Bible reveals there is to be another judgment at the end of time, the *general* or *last judgment*, where there is final victory over evil. As the Apostles' Creed puts it, "he will come to judge the living and the dead."

What is the particular judgment?
CCC 1021–1022; 1051

The Church teaches that each individual will immediately appear before God after death for a particular judgment. The particular judgment will reveal us for who we truly are. After death each of us will see his or her life as God sees it: a loving response to God or a self-centered turning away from God's love.

The Father of Jesus—our Father—is not a cruel, vindictive God. At the particular judgment God will judge us lovingly, mercifully, and justly. God's judgment will simply be a declaration of what is the truth about our acceptance or rejection of God.

What is the general or last judgment?
CCC 1038–1039; 1059

The general or last judgment is the time at which God will establish the heavenly community in its fullness. It will be preceded by the resurrection of the dead. At that time, the entire saving plan of God will be evident to everyone who ever lived. Jesus will serve as judge. His goodness, justice, mercy, and peace will establish God's reign in all its glory. People will recognize the sealing of their own destinies and their relationship to others. All will acknowledge and marvel at the majesty of the Lord.

> The Last Judgment will come when Christ returns
> in glory. . . . The Last Judgment will reveal that
> God's justice triumphs over all the injustices

committed by his creatures and that God's love is stronger than death.

—*Catechism of the Catholic Church*, 1040

What is the second coming of Christ?
CCC 1040–1041

Christians believe that God's reign has been established here on earth, but that it has not yet been fully realized. All Christians look for the day when Christ's work will be complete. The day of this glorious future will be the day when human history will come to a close, the day when Jesus Christ will come again. On this day the reign of God in all its eternal glory will be finally established.

When will Christ's second coming take place?
CCC 1041–1050; 1060

We do not know when the world will end and Jesus will come again in glory. The gospels (for example, Mark 13, Luke 21, and Matthew 24–25) and the book of Revelation use a special symbolic language, *apocalyptic language,* when writing about the end of the world and Jesus' second coming. This language should not be interpreted in a literal manner. Christians look forward to this day as a joyful encounter with the risen Lord, as a time when eternity and its promises of perfect happiness, joy, and peace will be fulfilled.

What the Church believes and teaches about the end of the world is that human history will come to a close at some time in the future. Jesus will come again at the *parousia,* a word that means "presence" or "arrival." When this takes place, at a time known to God alone, everyone who ever lived will recognize Jesus as Lord of all.

What do we believe about the resurrection of the body?
CCC 988–1004; 1015–1017

The resurrection of the body means that each person will be completely human—body and soul—for all eternity, sharing in the glorious life of our Lord Jesus Christ. St. Paul tells us that our resurrected bodies will be immortal, imperishable, glorious, powerful, and spiritual.

What is heaven?
CCC 1023–1029; 1053

Heaven is the state of eternal life in union with God and all those who share in his life. In heaven we will be given the "beatific vision," we will "see" God as God really is, and this seeing will bring us happiness. God made us to share the divine life; God made us for eternal happiness. Heaven is the final, perfect human fulfillment, a state of being that makes us wholly what we are meant to be—eternally filled with joy.

What is purgatory?
CCC 1030–1032; 1054–1055

The Church teaches that purgatory, a place or state of purification, exists as a preparation for entrance into heaven. The Church encourages us to pray, give alms, and do works of penance on behalf of those in purgatory.

Purgatory means "purification, cleansing." What we need cleansing of is any venial sin or any punishment due our sin that is present at death. In one sense, the process of purification takes place for the Christian each day he or she lives and attempts to rid himself or herself of sin and attachment to selfish concerns.

The Church has never defined the exact nature of purgatory—what kind of place or state of being purgatory is or how long it lasts. Some theologians suggest that when we see Christ's loving look, our own sinful infidelities agonize us to the degree that we have failed to respond to God's love. This encounter burns away or purifies our imperfection and opens us totally to the loving embrace of perfect union with God.

What is hell?
CCC 1033–1037; 1056–1058

Hell is eternal separation from God. In the New Testament, Jesus clearly stated its existence in a number of places. The Church teaches that there is a hell, but that the images employed by scripture to describe it are symbolic. They are attempts to describe the horror of an eternal life alienated from God and his love. This alienation extends to all interpersonal relationships. The person who dies having turned away freely and deliberately from God's redeeming love has chosen to live a life turned in on self—eternally. While we believe it is possible to definitively choose self over God and thus merit eternal punishment, we cannot state with certainty who in fact has made such a definitive choice. The person who loves God and translates that love into actions need not obsessively fear hell. Those who love God know that God is not out to get us. God gives us freedom, even if we sin. But we should never forget that he is a God of both mercy *and* justice.

21

The Church and Other Religions

Catholicism is the largest Christian denomination in the world and the largest branch of any of the world religions. We must be aware, however, that most of the world's population is not Christian. Millions of people belong to other religions. Yet they are our brothers and sisters too. Today the Church's attitude is one of profound respect and reverence toward other religions and those who practice them. Catholics and all Christians can and should gain much nourishment from respecting and learning about other religious traditions.

What are the major world religions?
CCC 839–842

The major world religions are typically divided into the religions of the West and the religions of the East. The religions of the West include Judaism and its two spiritual descendants: Christianity and Islam. Judaism defines itself as a religion of the covenant: Yahweh formed and sustained the Jewish people in return for their love and worship. Yahweh is their God, and Israel is God's people. Christianity professes that Jesus of Nazareth, a Jewish carpenter and teacher, is the Messiah, God's own Son, who fulfills all the promises made to Israel. Islam shares with Judaism and Christianity faith in one God. Though Islam acknowledges Jesus as a prophet and honors Mary his mother, it maintains that Mohammed is Allah's greatest prophet.

The religions of the East include Hinduism and Buddhism, which were born on the Indian subcontinent; Taoism in China; and the Shinto religions in Japan. To these major religions we could add numerous others, including the religions of Native Americans and those of the various aboriginal peoples of Australia, Africa, and the Arctic regions of the world.

What are the major Christian denominations?
CCC 834–838

Christianity is, numerically, the largest major world religion, with about one-third of Earth's population identifying themselves as Christian. There are three major groupings within Christianity: Catholic, Orthodox, and Protestant.

Catholicism, the largest Christian denomination, includes those Christians who acknowledge the primacy of the pope.

The Orthodox are those churches (notably the Greek and Russian Orthodox Churches) that are historically separated from Rome—that is, not in union with the pope. Of all Christian groups, the Orthodox are closest to Roman Catholicism in faith, theology, and Church structures.

The Reformation of the sixteenth century resulted in the formation of the mainstream Protestant communities, beginning with Lutherans and now including Methodists, Baptists, and Presbyterians, to name a few. These denominations share many beliefs in common with Catholics, notably the articles of faith in the Nicene Creed, but they differ on other points of belief and practice.

What is ecumenism?
CCC 816; 820–822

Ecumenism comes from a Greek word that means "universal." It refers to the active effort to restore unity among all Christians—a gift of Christ and calling of the Holy Spirit. The *Decree on Ecumenism* of the Second Vatican Council provides the Church with a mandate and the necessary guidance to engage in this dynamic process of theological and doctrinal dialogue, good will, and deep prayer.

Work on behalf of ecumenism does not mean that the Catholic Church denies its unique role in God's plan of salvation. Catholics believe that the fullness of the truth and grace of Jesus Christ can be found in—subsists in— the Roman Catholic Church. Nevertheless, the Church also teaches that the Holy Spirit works in all people of good will in order to build up God's kingdom. Other Christian communities share in the building up of the kingdom to the degree that they are related to the one true Church of Jesus Christ.

How can the individual Christian work toward Christian unity?
CCC 821

A primary duty of Catholics in the work for unity is to make sure that the Catholic Church itself is living the Gospel message in fidelity to Jesus Christ. Furthermore, Catholics can acknowledge the spiritual gifts that our Lord has endowed on our Christian brothers and sisters and allow their faith, hope, and love to inspire us. In addition, we can do the following:

- *Pray.* We can pray for Christian unity, asking the Spirit to guide our efforts, and pray with our Christian brothers and sisters for the needs of one another and the world.

- *Study.* We have a duty to know better the depths of our own faith and to appreciate the meaning of Church doctrines so that we can help others to understand them as well. Knowledge of other religions can also be very helpful for mutual understanding.

- *Communicate.* As individuals we can share our own Catholic beliefs and engage in open exchanges with members of other faiths as occasions arise. The Second Vatican Council encourages us to eliminate prejudicial language from our conversation.

- *Cooperate.* The Church calls on us to work together with our Christian brothers and sisters of other communions on projects of social action. Putting the Gospel into action in joint efforts of Christian charity can go a long way in bringing Christians together.

22

Being Catholic

As we conclude this overview of Catholicism, let us never forget that to be a member of the Lord's body is indeed a privilege and a lifelong journey. The privilege of being called to belong to the Church brings with it major responsibilities. The Lord has chosen us to do his work. Our task is to share the Good News of Jesus Christ, the way to the Father, with all spiritual travelers.

Who is a Catholic?

- A Catholic is a Christian who belongs to a faith community that shares Jesus' vision and responds to his presence in our midst. A Catholic loves each member of this community and uses his or her unique talents to contribute to it in a positive way.

- A Catholic believes in God, our loving Father. This loving Father has made us brothers and sisters to everyone who has ever lived. Moreover, he has sent us his Son, Jesus Christ, who won for us our salvation and gave us eternal life.

- A Catholic acknowledges the divinity of Jesus Christ, God's Son, our Lord and Savior.

- A Catholic believes in the Holy Spirit and the Spirit's powerful presence in the Church and in the world. A Catholic accepts and uses the many gifts the Spirit showers on us. It is the Holy Spirit who enables a Catholic to accept Jesus into his or her life.

- A Catholic attempts to live in harmony with Jesus' teaching: loving God above all things; loving neighbors, as oneself; forgiving enemies; extending special care to the poor, the lonely, and the outcast.

- A Catholic works for peace and justice, thus helping the Lord promote the spread of his reign on earth as it is in heaven.

- A Catholic commemorates the paschal mystery by living a sacramental life. This includes, for example, recognizing a need for forgiveness through the celebration of the Sacrament of Reconciliation.

- A Catholic cherishes the Eucharist as a special sign of God's nourishing love and a privileged way to encounter the living Lord Jesus. A Catholic participates fully in the Eucharist every Sunday.

- A Catholic makes time to develop a prayer life, because prayer leads to an intimate friendship with the Lord.

- A Catholic reveres and reads the Bible, which contains the Word of God.

- A Catholic acknowledges the role of proper authority in the Church—for example, by seeking guidance for moral decisions from the Church's official teachers.

- A Catholic serves others by imitating Jesus who washed the feet of his disciples and commanded us to do the same.

- A Catholic proclaims the Gospel, thus publicly acknowledging Jesus Christ and his Church. A Catholic is willing to stand up to ridicule and suffering in the service of the Gospel truth.

- A Catholic seeks to emulate Mary—the Mother of God and the Mother of the Church—and esteems the saints as models of how to live the Christian life.

- A Catholic is fiercely committed to the protection of human life from conception to natural death. In a special way, a Catholic defends innocent human life by opposing abortion, war, assisted suicide, abject poverty, and other assaults on human life.

- A Catholic belongs to Jesus Christ, his Church, and the world to which they proclaim in word and deed the Good News of our gracious, loving Savior.

Traditional Prayers

Sign of the Cross
In the name of the Father, and of the Son,
and of the Holy Spirit. Amen.

Our Father
Our Father
who art in heaven,
hallowed be thy name;
thy kingdom come,
thy will be done
on earth as it is in heaven.
Give us this day our daily bread,
and forgive us our trespasses,
as we forgive those who trespass against us;
and lead us not into temptation,
but deliver us from evil.

Frequently this simple doxology is added:
For the kingdom,
the power, and the glory are yours
now and forever.
Amen.

Glory Be
Glory be to the Father
and to the Son
and to the Holy Spirit,
as it was in the beginning,
is now, and will be forever. Amen.

Hail Mary

Hail Mary, full of grace,
the Lord is with you.
Blessed are you among women
and blessed is the fruit of your womb, Jesus.
Holy Mary, Mother of God,
pray for us sinners now
and at the hour of our death. Amen.

The Apostles' Creed

I believe in God,
the Father almighty,
Creator of heaven and earth,
and in Jesus Christ, his only Son, our Lord.

Who was conceived by the Holy Spirit,
born of the Virgin Mary,
suffered under Pontius Pilate,
was crucified, died, and was buried;
he descended into hell;
on the third day he rose again from the dead;
he ascended into heaven,
and is seated at the right hand of God the Father almighty;
from there he will come to judge the living and the dead.

I believe in the Holy Spirit,
the holy catholic Church,
the communion of saints,
the forgiveness of sins,
the resurrection of the body,
and life everlasting. Amen.

Act of Contrition

O my God,
I am sorry for my sins with all my heart.
In choosing to do wrong and failing to do good,
I have sinned against you whom I should love
above all things.
I firmly intend, with your help, to do penance,
to sin no more,
and to avoid whatever leads me to sin.
Our Savior Jesus Christ suffered and died for us.
In his name, my God, have mercy. Amen.

Grace before Meals

Bless us, O Lord,
and these your gifts,
which we are about to receive from your bounty,
through Christ our Lord. Amen.

Prayer after Meals

We give you thanks, almighty God,
for these and all the gifts,
which we have received
from your goodness,
through Christ our Lord. Amen.

Prayer for the Faithful Departed

Eternal rest grant unto them, O Lord.
R: And let perpetual light shine upon them.
May their souls and the souls of all the faithful
departed, through the mercy of God, rest in peace.
R: Amen.

Peace Prayer of St. Francis

Lord, make me an instrument of your peace.
Where there is hatred, let me sow love;
where there is injury, pardon;
where there is doubt, faith;
where there is despair, hope;
where there is darkness, light;
where there is sadness, joy.

O Divine Master,
grant that I may not seek so much to be consoled,
as to console;
to be understood, as to understand;
to be loved, as to love.
For it is in giving that we receive,
it is in pardoning that we are pardoned,
and it is in dying that we are born to eternal life.
Amen.

Michael Francis Pennock (1945–2009) was the author of several bestselling textbooks for Catholic high schools, including *Encountering Jesus in the New Testament, Your Life in Christ, Our Catholic Faith*, and three recent texts to support the new USCCB high school curriculum framework.

Pennock taught theology for more than thirty-five years, mostly at his beloved alma mater, St. Ignatius High School in Cleveland, Ohio. His students, numbering more than fifteen thousand, continue to pour out their remembrances and support for the man they called "Doc Pennock."

Founded in 1865, Ave Maria Press,
a ministry of the Congregation of
Holy Cross, is a Catholic publishing
company that serves the spiritual and
formative needs of the Church and its
schools, institutions, and ministers;
Christian individuals and families; and
others seeking spiritual nourishment.

For a complete listing of titles from

Ave Maria Press

Sorin Books

Forest of Peace

Christian Classics

visit www.avemariapress.com

ave maria press® / Notre Dame, IN 46556
A Ministry of the United States Province of Holy Cross